The Picture by Philip Massinger

Philip Massinger was baptized at St. Thomas's in Salisbury on November 24th, 1583.

Massinger is described in his matriculation entry at St. Alban Hall, Oxford (1602), as the son of a gentleman. His father, who had also been educated there, was a member of parliament, and attached to the household of Henry Herbert, 2nd Earl of Pembroke. The Earl was later seen as a potential patron for Massinger.

He left Oxford in 1606 without a degree. His father had died in 1603, and accounts suggest that Massinger was left with no financial support this, together with rumours that he had converted to Catholicism, meant the next stage of his career needed to provide an income.

Massinger went to London to make his living as a dramatist, but he is only recorded as author some fifteen years later, when The Virgin Martyr (1621) is given as the work of Massinger and Thomas Dekker.

During those early years as a playwright he wrote for the Elizabethan stage entrepreneur, Philip Henslowe. It was a difficult existence. Poverty was always close and there was constant pleading for advance payments on forthcoming works merely to survive.

After Henslowe died in 1616 Massinger and John Fletcher began to write primarily for the King's Men and Massinger would write regularly for them until his death.

The tone of the dedications in later plays suggests evidence of his continued poverty. In the preface of The Maid of Honour (1632) he wrote, addressing Sir Francis Foljambe and Sir Thomas Bland: "I had not to this time subsisted, but that I was supported by your frequent courtesies and favours."

The prologue to The Guardian (1633) refers to two unsuccessful plays and two years of silence, when the author feared he had lost popular favour although, from the little evidence that survives, it also seems he had involved some of his plays with political characters which would have cast shadows upon England's alliances.

Philip Massinger died suddenly at his house near the Globe Theatre on March 17th, 1640. He was buried the next day in the churchyard of St. Saviour's, Southwark, on March 18th, 1640. In the entry in the parish register he is described as a "stranger," which, however, implies nothing more than that he belonged to another parish.

Index of Contents

DRAMATIS PERSONAE
Ladislaus, king of Hungary
Ferdinand, general of the army
Eubulus, an old counsellor
Mathias, a knight of Bohemia
Ubaldo }
Ricardo } wild courtiers
Julio Baptista, a great scholar
Hilario, servant to Sophia
Two Boys, representing Apollo and Pallas
Two Couriers
A Guide
Servants to the queen
Servants to Mathias
Honoria, the queen
Sophia, wife to Mathias
Corisca, Sophia's woman
Maskers, Attendants, Officers, Captains, &c.

SCENE: Partly in Hungary, and partly in Bohemia.

THE PICTURE

SCENE I. The Frontiers of Bohemia

Enter **MATHIAS**, **SOPHIA**, **CORISCA**, **HILARIO**, with other **SERVANTS**

MATHIAS
Since we must part, Sophia, to pass further
Is not alone impertinent, but dangerous.
We are not distant from the Turkish camp
Above five leagues, and who knows but some party
Of his Timariots, that scour the country,
May fall upon us? be now, as thy name,
Truly interpreted, hath ever spoke thee,
Wise, and discreet; and to thy understanding
Marry thy constant patience.

SOPHIA
You put me, sir,
To the utmost trial of it.

MATHIAS
Nay, no melting;
Since the necessity that now separates us,
We have long since disputed, and the reasons
Forcing me to it, too oft wash'd in tears.
I grant that you, in birth, were far above me,
And great men, my superiors, rivals for you;
But mutual consent of heart, as hands,
Join'd by true love, hath made us one, and equal:
Nor is it in me mere desire of fame,
Or to be cried up by the public voice,
For a brave soldier, that puts on my armour:
Such airy tumours take not me. You know
How narrow our demeans are, and what's more,
Having as yet no charge of children on us;
We hardly can subsist.

SOPHIA
In you alone, sir,
I have all abundance.

MATHIAS
For my mind's content,
In your own language I could answer you.
You have been an obedient wife, a right one;
And to my power, though short of your desert,
I have been ever an indulgent husband.

We have long enjoy 'd the sweets of love, and though
Not to satiety, or loathing, yet
We must not live such dotards on our pleasures,
As still to hug them, to the certain loss
Of profit and preferment. Competent means
Maintains a quiet bed; want breeds dissention,
Even in good women.

SOPHIA

Have you found in me, sir,
Any distaste, or sign of discontent,
For want of what's superfluous?

MATHIAS

No, Sophia;
Nor shalt thou ever have cause to repent
Thy constant course in goodness, if heaven bless
My honest undertakings. 'Tis for thee
That I turn soldier, and put forth, dearest,
Upon this sea of action, as a factor,
To trade for rich materials to adorn
Thy noble parts, and shew them in full lustre.
I blush that other ladies, less in beauty
And outward form, but in the harmony
Of the soul's ravishing music, the same age
Not to be named with thee, should so outshine thee
In jewels, and variety of wardrobes;
While you, to whose sweet innocence both Indies
Compared are of no value, wanting these,
Pass unregarded.

SOPHIA

If I am so rich, or
In your opinion, why should you borrow
Additions for me?

MATHIAS

Why! I should be censured
Of ignorance, possessing such a jewel
Above all price, if I forbear to give it
The best of ornaments: therefore, Sophia,
In few words know my pleasure, and obey me,
As you have ever done. To your discretion
Leave the government of my family,
And our poor fortunes; and from these command
Obedience to you, as to myself:
To the utmost of what's mine, live plentifully;
And, ere the remnant of our store be spent,

With my good sword I hope I shall reap for you
A harvest in such full abundance, as
Shall make a merry winter.

SOPHIA
Since you are not
To be diverted, sir, from what you purpose,
All arguments to stay you here are useless:
Go when you please, sir. Eyes, I charge you waste not
One drop of sorrow; look you hoard all up
Till in my widow'd bed I call upon you,
But then be sure you fail not. You blest angels,
Guardians of human life, I at this instant
Forbear t'invoke you: at our parting, 'twere
To personate devotion. My soul
Shall go along with you, and, when you are
Circled with death and horror, seek and find you;
And then I will not leave a saint unsued to
For your protection. To tell you what
I will do in your absence, would shew poorly;
My actions shall speak for me: 'twere to doubt you,
To beg I may hear from you; where you are
You cannot live obscure, nor shall one post,
By night or day, pass unexamined by me.
If I dwell long upon your lips, consider,

[Kisses him.

After this feast, the griping fast that follows,
And it will be excusable; pray turn from me.
All that I can, is spoken.

[Exit.

MATHIAS
Follow your mistress.
Forbear your wishes for me; let me find them,
At my return, in your prompt will to serve her.

HILARIO
For my part, sir, I will grow lean with study
To make her merry.

CORISCA
Though you are my lord,
Yet being her gentlewoman, by my place
I may take my leave; your hand, or, if you please
To have me fight so high, I'll not be coy,

But stand a-tip-toe for't.

MATHIAS
O farewell, girl!

[Kisses her.

HILARIO
A kiss well begg'd, Corisca.

CORISCA
'Twas my fee;
Love, how he melts! I cannot blame my lady's
Unwillingness to part with such marmalade lips.
There will be scrambling for them in the camp;
And were it not for my honesty, I could wish now
I were his leaguer laundress; I would find
Soap of mine own, enough to wash his linen,
Or I would strain hard for't.

HILARIO
How the mammet twitters!
Come, come; my lady stays for us.

CORISCA
Would I had been
Her ladyship the last night!

HILARIO
No more of that, wench.

[Exeunt **HILARIO**, **CORISCA**, and the rest.

MATHIAS
I am strangely troubled, yet why I should nourish
A fury here, and with imagined food,
Having no real grounds on which to raise
A building of suspicion she was ever
Or can be false hereafter. I in this
But foolishly enquire the knowledge of
A future sorrow, which, if I find out,
My present ignorance were a cheap purchase,
Though with my loss of being. I have already
Dealt with a friend of mine, a general scholar,
One deeply read in nature's hidden secrets,
And, though with much unwillingness, have won him
To do as much as art can, to resolve me
My fate that follows to my wish, he's come.

[Enter **BAPTISTA**.

Julio Baptista, now I may affirm
Your promise and performance walk together;
And therefore, without circumstance, to the point:
Instruct me what I am.

BAPTISTA
I could wish you had
Made trial of my love some other way.

MATHIAS
Nay, this is from the purpose.

BAPTISTA
If you can
Proportion your desire to any mean,
I do pronounce you happy; I have found
By certain rules of art, your matchless wife
Is to this present hour from all pollution
Free, and untainted.

MATHIAS
Good.

BAPTISTA
In reason, therefore,
You should fix here, and make no further search
Of what may fall hereafter.

MATHIAS
O, Baptista,
'Tis not in me to master so my passions;
I must "know further, or you have made good
But half your promise. While my love stood by,
Holding her upright, and my presence was
A watch upon her, her desires being met too
With equal ardour from me, what one proof
Could she give of her constancy, being untempted?
But when I am absent, and my coming back
Uncertain, and those wanton heats in women,
Not to be quench 'd by lawful means, and she
The absolute disposer of herself,
Without control or curb; nay, more, invited
By opportunity, and all strong temptations,
If then she hold out

BAPTISTA

As, no doubt, she will.

MATHIAS

Those doubts must be made certainties, Baptista,
By your assurance; or your boasted art
Deserves no admiration. How you trifle,
And play with my affliction! I am on
The rack, till you confirm me.

BAPTISTA

Sure, Mathias,
I am no god, nor can I dive into
Her hidden thoughts, or know what her intents are;
That is denied to art, and kept conceal'd
E'en from the devils themselves: they can but guess,
Out of long observation, what is likely;
But positively to fortel that shall be,
You may conclude impossible. All I can,
I will do for you; when you are distant from her
A thousand leagues, as if you then were with her,
You shall know truly when she is solicited,
And how far wrought on.

MATHIAS

I desire no more.

BAPTISTA

Take then this little model of Sophia,
With more than human skill limn'd to the life;

[Gives him a picture.

Each line and lineament of it, in the drawing,
So punctually observed, that, had it motion,
In so much 'twere herself.

MATHIAS

It is, indeed,
An admirable piece! but if it have not
Some hidden virtue that I cannot guess at,
In what can it advantage me?

BAPTISTA

I'll instruct you:
Carry it still about you, and as oft
As you desire to know how she's affected,
With curious eyes peruse it: while it keeps

The figure it now has, entire and perfect,
She is not only innocent in fact,
But unattempted; but if once it vary
From the true form, and what's now white and red
Incline to yellow, rest most confident
She's with all violence courted, but unconquer'd;
But if it turn all black, 'tis an assurance
The fort, by composition or surprise,
Is forced, or with her free consent surrender'd.

MATHIAS
How much you have engaged me for this favour,
The service of my whole life shall make good.

BAPTISTA
We will not part so, I'll along with you,
And it is needful: with the rising sun,
The armies meet; yet, ere the fight begin,.
In spite of opposition, I will place you
In the head of the Hungarian general's troop.
And near his person.

MATHIAS
As my better angel,
You shall direct and guide me.

BAPTISTA
As we ride
I'll tell you more.

MATHIAS
In all things I'll obey you.

[Exeunt.

SCENE II. Hungary. Alba Regalis

A State-room in the Palace.

Enter **UBALDO** and **RICARDO**.

RICARDO
When came the post?

UBALDO
The last night.

RICARDO
From the camp?

UBALDO
Yes, as 'tis said, and the letter writ and sign'd
By the general, Ferdinand.

RICARDO
Nay, then, sans question,
It is of moment.

UBALDO
It concerns the lives
Of two great armies.

RICARDO
Was it cheerfully
Received by the king?

UBALDO
Yes; for being assured
The armies were in view of one another,
Having proclaim'd a public fast and prayer
For the good success, he dispatch'd a gentleman
Of his privy chamber to the general
With absolute authority from him,
To try the fortune of a day.

RICARDO
No doubt then
The general will come on, and fight it bravely.
Heaven prosper him! This military art,
I grant to be the noblest of professions;
And yet, I thank my stars for't, I was never
Inclined to learn it: since this bubble honour
(Which is, indeed, the nothing soldiers fight for,)
With the loss of limbs or life, is, in my judgment,
Too dear a purchase.

UBALDO
Give me our court warfare:
The danger is not great in the encounter^
Of a fair mistress.

RICARDO
Fair and sound together
Do very well, Ubaldo; but such are,

With difficulty, to be found out; and when they know
Their value, prized too high. By thy own report,
Thou wast at twelve a gamester, and since that,
Studied all kinds of females, from the night-trader
I' the street, with certain danger to thy pocket,
To the great lady in her cabinet;
That spent upon thee more in cullises,
To strengthen thy weak back, than would maintain
Twelve Flanders mares, and as many running horses:
Besides apothecaries and surgeons' bills,
Paid upon all occasions, and those frequent.

UBALDO
You talk, Ricardo, as if yet you were
A novice in those mysteries.

RICARDO
By no means;
My doctor can assure the contrary:
I lose no time. I have felt the pain and pleasure,
As he that is a gamester, and plays often,
Must sometimes be a loser.

UBALDO
Wherefore, then,
Do you envy me?

RICARDO
It grows not from my want,
Nor thy abundance; but being, as I am,
The likelier man, and of much more experience,
My good parts are my curses: there's no beauty,
But yields ere it be summon'd; and, as nature
Had sign'd me the monopoly of maidenheads,
There's none can buy till I have made my market.
Satiety cloys me; as I live, I would part with
Half my estate, nay, travel o'er the world,
To find that only phcenix in my search,
That could hold out against me.

UBALDO
Be not rapt so;
You may spare that labour. As she is a. woman,
What think you of the queen?

RICARDO
I dare not aim at
The petticoat royal, that is still excepted:

Yet, were she not my king's, being the abstract.
Of all that's rare, or to bewish'd in woman,
To write her in my catalogue, having enjoy 'd her,
I would venture my neck to a halter but we talk of
Impossibilities: as she hath a beauty
Would make old Nestor young; such majesty
Draws forth a sword of terror to defend it,
As would fright Paris, though the queen of love
Vow'd her best furtherance to him.

UBALDO
Have you observed
The gravity of her language, mix'd with sweetness?

RICARDO
Then, at what distance she reserves herself,
When the king himself makes his approaches to her

UBALDO
As she were still a virgin, and his life
But one continued wooing.

RICARDO
She well knows
Her worth, and values it.

UBALDO
And so far the king is
Indulgent to her humours, that he forbears
The duty of a husband, but when she calls for't.

RICARDO
All his imaginations and thoughts
Are buried in her; the loud noise of war
Cannot awake him.

UBALDO
At this very instant,
When both his life and crown are at the stake,
He only studies her content, and when
She's pleased to show herself, music and masques
Are with all care and cost provided for her.

RICARDO
This night she promised to appear.

UBALDO
You may

Believe it by the diligence of the king,
As if he were her harbinger.

[Enter **LADISLAUS**, **EUBULUS** and **ATTENDANTS** with perfumes.

LADISLAUS
These rooms
Are not perfumed, as we directed,

EUBULUS
Not, sir!
I know not what you would have; I am sure the smoak
Cost treble the price of the whole week's provision
Spent in your majesty's kitchens.

LADISLAUS
How I scorn
Thy gross comparison! When my Honoria,
The amazement of the present time, and envy
Of all succeeding ages, does descend
To sanctify a place, and in her presence
Makes it a temple to me, can I be
Too curious, much less prodigal to receive her?
But that the splendour of her beams of beauty
Hath struck thee blind

EUBULUS
As dotage hath done you.

LADISLAUS
Dotage? O blasphemy! is it in me
To serve her to her merit? Is she not
The daughter of a king?

EUBULUS
And you the son
Of ours, I take it; by what privilege else,
Do you reign over us? for my part, I know not
I Where the disparity lies.

LADISLAUS
Her birth, old man,
'Old in the kingdom's service, which protects thee,
Is the least grace in her: and though her beauties
Might make the Thunderer a rival for her,
They are but superficial ornaments,
And faintly speak her: from her heavenly mind,
Were all antiquity and fiction lost,

Our modern poets could not, in their fancy,
But fashion a Minerva far transcending
The imagined one whom Homer only dreamt of.
But then add this, she's mine, mine, Eubulus!
And though she knows one glance from her fair eyes
Must make all gazers her idolaters,
She is so sparing of their influence
That, to shun superstition in others,
She shoots her powerful beams only at me.
And can I, then, whom she desires to hold
Her kingly captive above all the world,
Whose nations and empires, if she pleased,
She might command as slaves, but gladly pay
The humble tribute of my love and service,
Nay, if I said of adoration, to her,
I did not err?

EUBULUS
Well, since you hug your fetters,
In Love's name wear them! You are a king, and that
Concludes you wise: your will a powerful reason,
Which we, that are foolish subjects, must not argue.
And what in a mean man I should call folly,
Is in your majesty remarkable wisdom:
But for me, I subscribe.

LADISLAUS
Do, and look up,
Upon this wonder.

[Loud music.

[Enter **HONORIA** in state, under a Canopy; her train borne up by **SYLVIA** and **ACANTHE**.

RICARDO
Wonder! It is more, sir.

UBALDO
A rapture, an astonishment.

RICARDO
What think you, sir?

EUBULUS
As the king thinks; that is the surest guard
We courtiers ever lie at. Was prince ever
So drown'd in dotage? Without spectacles
I can see a handsome woman, and she is so:

But yet to admiration look not on her.
Heaven, how he fawns! and, as it were his duty,
With what assured gravity she receives it!
Her hand again! O she at length vouchsafes
Her lip, and as he had sucked nectar from it,
How he's exalted! Women in their natures
Affect command; but this humility
In a husband and a king, marks her the way
To absolute tyranny.

[The **KING** seats her on his throne.

So! Juno's placed
In Jove's tribunal: and, like Mercury,
(Forgetting his own greatness,) he attends
For her employments. She prepares to speak;
What oracles shall we hear now? [Aside.

HONORIA
That you please, sir,
With such assurances of love and favour,
To grace your handmaid, but in being yours, sir,
A matchless queen, and one that knows herself so,
Binds me in retribution to deserve
The grace conferr'd upon me.

LADISLAUS
You transcend
In all things excellent: and it is my glory,
Your worth weigh'd truly, to depose myself
From absolute command, surrendering up
My will and faculties to your disposure:
And here I vow, not for a day or year,
But my whole life, which I wish long, to serve you,
That whatsoever I, in justice, may
Exact from these my subjects, you from me
May boldly challenge: and when you require it,
In sign of my subjection, as your vassal,
Thus I will pay my homage.

HONORIA
O forbear, sir!
Let not my lips envy my robe; on them
Print your allegiance often: I desire
No other fealty.

LADISLAUS
Gracious sovereign!

Boundless in bounty!

EUBULUS
Is not here fine fooling!
He's questionless, bewitch'd. Would I were gelt,
So that would disenchant him! though I forfeit
My life for't, I must speak. By your good leave, sir

[Passing before the **KING**.

I have no suit to you, nor can you grant one,
Having no power: you are like me, a subject,
Her more than serene majesty being present.
And I must tell you, 'tis ill manners in you,
Having deposed yourself, to keep your hat on,
And not stand bare, as we do, being no king,
But a fellow-subject with us. Gentlemen-ushers,
It does belong to your place, see it reform'd;
He has given away his crown, and cannot challenge
The privilege of his bonnet.

LADISLAUS
Do not tempt me.

EUBULUS
Tempt you! in what? in following your example?
If you are angry, question me hereafter,
As Ladislaus should do Eubulus,
On equal terms. You were of late my sovereign,
But weary of it, I now bend my knee
To her divinity, and desire a boon
From her more than magnificence.

HONORIA
Take it freely.
Nay, be not moved; for our mirth's sake let us hear him.

EUBULUS
'Tis but to ask a question: Have you ne'er read
The story of Semiramis and Ninus?

HONORIA
Not as I remember.

EUBULUS
I will then instruct you,
And 'tis to the purpose: This Ninus was a king,
And such an impotent loving king as this was,

But now he's none; this Ninus (pray you observe me)
Doted on this Semiramis, a smith's wife;
(I must confess, there the comparison holds not,
You are a king's daughter, yet, under your correction,
Like her, a woman;) this Assyrian monarch,
Of whom this is a pattern, to express
His love and service, seated her, as you are,
In his regal throne, and bound by oath his nobles,
Forgetting all allegiance to himself,
One day to be her subjects, and to put
In execution whatever she
Pleased to impose upon them: pray you command him
To minister the like to us, and then
You shall hear what follow'd.

LADISLAUS
Well, sir, to your story.

EUBULUS
You have no warrant, stand by; let me know
Your pleasure, goddess.

HONORIA
Let this nod assure you.

EUBULUS
Goddess-like, indeed! as I live, a pretty idol!
She knowing her power, wisely made use of it;
And fearing his inconstancy, and repentance
Of what he had granted, (as, in reason, madam,
You may do his,) that he might never have
Power to recall his grant, or question her
For her short government, instantly gave order
To have his head struck off.

LADISLAUS
Is't possible?

EUBULUS
The story says so, and commends her wisdom
For making use of her authority.
And it is worth your imitation, madam:
He loves subjection, and you are no queen,
Unless you make him feel the weight of it.
You are more than all the world to him, and that
He may be so to you, and not seek change,
When his delights are sated, mew him up
In some close prison, (if you let him live,

Which is no policy,) and there diet him
As you think fit, to feed your appetite;
Since there ends his ambition.

UBALDO
Devilish counsel!

RICARDO
The king's amazed.

UBALDO
The queen appears, too, full
Of deep imaginations; Eubulus
Hath put both to it.

RICARDO
Now she seems resolved:
I long to know the issue.

[**HONORIA** descends from the throne.

HONORIA
Give me leave,
Dear sir, to reprehend you for appearing
Perplex'd with what this old man, out of envy
Of your unequal graces shower'd upon me,
Hath, in his fabulous story, saucily
Applied to me. Sir, that you only nourish
One doubt Honoria dares abuse the power
With which she is invested by your favour;
Or that she ever can make use of it
To the injury of you, the great bestower,
Takes from your judgment. It was your delight
To seek to me with more obsequiousness
Than I desired: and stood it with my duty
Not to receive what you were pleased to offer?
I do but act the part you put upon me,
And though you make me personate a queen,
And you my subject, when the play, your pleasure,
Is at a period, I am what I was
Before I enter'd, still your humble wife,
And you my royal sovereign.

RICARDO
Admirable!

HONORIA
I have heard of captains taken more with dangers

Than the rewards; and if, in your approaches
To those delights which are your own, and freely,
To heighten your desire, you make the passage
Narrow and difficult, shall I prescribe you,
Or blame your fondness? or can that swell me
Beyond my just proportion?

UBALDO
Above wonder!

LADISLAUS
Heaven make me thankful for such goodness!

HONORIA
Now, sir,
The state I took to satisfy your pleasure,
I change to this humility; and the oath
You made to me of homage, I thus cancel,
And seat you in your own.

[Leads the **KING** to the throne.

LADISLAUS
I am transported
Beyond myself.

HONORIA
And now, to your wise lordship:
Am I proved a Semiramis? or hath
My Ninus, as maliciously you made him,
Cause to repent the excess of favour to me,
Which you call dotage?

LADISLAUS
Answer, wretch!

EUBULUS
I dare, sir,
And say, however the event may plead
In your defence, you had a guilty cause;
Nor was it wisdom in you, I repeat it,
To teach a lady, humble in herself,
With the ridiculous dotage of a lover,
'To be ambitious.

HONORIA
Eubulus, I am so;
Tis rooted in me; you mistake my temper.

I do profess myself to be the most
Ambitious of my sex, but not to hold
Command over my lord; such a proud torrent
Would sink me in my wishes: not that I
Am ignorant how much I can deserve,
And may with justice challenge.

EUBULUS
This I look'd for;
After this seeming humble ebb, I knew
A gushing tide would follow. [Aside.

HONORIA
By my birth,
And liberal gifts of nature, as of fortune,
From you, as things beneath me, I expect
What's due to majesty, in which I am
A sharer with your sovereign.

EUBULUS
Good again!

HONORIA
And as I am most eminent in place,
In all my actions I would appear so.

LADISLAUS
You need not fear a rival.

HONORIA
I hope not;
And till I find one, I disdain to know
What envy is.

LADISLAUS
You' are above it, madam.

HONORIA
For beauty without art, discourse, and free
From affectation, with what graces else
Can in the wife and daughter of a king
Be wish'd, I dare prefer myself, as

EUBULUS
I blush for you, lady. Trumpet your own praises!
This spoken by the people had been heard
With honour to you. Does the court afford
No oil-tongued parasite, that you are forced

To be your own gross flatterer?

LADISLAUS
Be dumb,
Thou spirit of contradiction!

HONORIA
The wolf
But barks against the moon, and I contemn it.
The mask you promised.

[A horn sounded within.

LADISLAUS
Let them enter.

[Enter a **COURIER**.

How!

EUBULUS
Here's one, I fear, unlook'd for.

LADISLAUS
From the camp?

COURIER
The general, victorious in your fortune,
Kisses your hand in this, sir. "

[Delivers a letter.

LADISLAUS
That great Power,
Who at his pleasure does dispose of battles,
Be ever praised for't! Read, sweet, and partake it:
The Turk is vanquish'd, and with little loss
Upon our part, in which our joy is doubled.

EUBULUS
But let it not exalt you; bear it, sir,
With moderation, and pay what you owe for't.

LADISLAUS
I understand thee, Eubulus. I'll not now
Enquire particulars.

[Exit **COURIER**.

Our delights deferr'd,
With reverence to the temples; there we'll tender
Our souls' devotions to his dread might,
Who edged our swords, and taught us how to fight.

[Exeunt.

SCENE I. Bohemia. A Hall in Mathias' House

Enter **HILARIO** and **CORISCA**.

HILARIO
You like my speech?

CORISCA
Yes, if you give it action
In the delivery.

HILARIO
If! I pity you.
I have play'd the fool before; this is not the first time,
Nor shall be, I hope, the last.

CORISCA
Nay, I think so too.

HILARIO
And if I put her not out of her dumps with laughter,
I'll make her howl for anger.

CORISCA
Not too much
Of that, good fellow Hilario: our sad lady
Hath drank too often of that bitter cup;
A pleasant one must restore her. With what patience
Would she endure to hear of the death of my lord;
That, merely out of doubt he may miscarry,
I Afflicts herself thus?

HILARIO
Umph! 'tis a question
A widow only can resolve. There be some
That in their husband's sicknesses have wept

Their pottle of tears a day; but being once certain
At midnight he was dead, have in the morning
Dried up their handkerchiefs, and thought no more on't.

CORISCA
Tush, she is none of that race; if her sorrow
Be not true and perfect, I, against my sex.
Will take my oath woman ne'er wept in earnest.
She has made herself a prisoner to her chamber,
Dark as a dungeon, in which no beam
Of comfort enters. She admits no visits;
Eats little, and her nightly music is
Of sighs and groans, tuned to such harmony
Of feeling grief, that I, against my nature,
Am made one of the consort. This hour only
She takes the air, a custom every day
She solemnly observes, with greedy hopes,
From some that pass by, to receive assurance
Of the success and safety of her lord.
Now, if that your device will take

HILARIO
Ne'er fear it:
I am provided cap-a-pie, and have
My properties in readiness.

SOPHIA [within]
Bring my veil, there.

CORISCA
Begone, I hear her coming.

HILARIO
If I do not
Appear, and, what's more, appear perfect, hiss me.

[Exit.

[Enter **SOPHIA**.

SOPHIA
I was flatter'd once, I was a star, but now
Turn'd a prodigious meteor, and, like one,
Hang in the air between my hopes and fears;
And every hour, the little stuff burnt out
That yields a waning light to dying comfort,
I do expect my fall, and certain ruin.
In wretched things more wretched is delay;

And Hope, a parasite to me, being unmaskd,
Appears more horrid than Despair, and my
Distraction worse than madness. Even my prayers,
When with most zeal sent upward, are pull'd down
With strong imaginary doubts and fears,
And in their sudden precipice o'erwhelm me.
Dreams and fantastic visions walk the round
About my widow'd bed, and every slumber's;
Broken with loud alarms: can these be then
But sad presages, girl?

CORISCA
You make them so,
And antedate a loss shall ne'er fall on you.
Such pure affection, such mutual love,
A bed, and undefiled on either part,
A house without contention, in two bodies
One will and soul, like to the rod of concord,
Kissing each other, cannot be short-lived,
Or end in barrenness. If all these, dear madam,
(Sweet in your sadness,) should produce no fruit,
Or leave the age no models of yourselves,
To witness to posterity what you were;
Succeeding times, frighted with the example,
But hearing of your story, would instruct
Their faires issue to meet sensually,
Like other creatures, and forbear to raise
True Love, or Hymen, altars.

SOPHIA
O Corisca,
I know thy reasons are like to thy wishes;
And they are built upon a weak foundation,
To raise me comfort. Ten long days are past,
Ten long days, my Corisca, since my lord
Embark'd himself upon a sea of danger,
In his dear care of me. And if his life
Had not been shipwreck'd on the rock of war,
His tenderness of me (knowing how much
I languish for his absence) had provided
Some trusty friend, from whom I might receive
Assurance of his safety.

CORISCA
Ill news, madam,
Are swallow-wing 'd, but what's good walks on crutches:
With patience expect it, and, ere long,
No doubt you shall hear from him.

[A horn without.

SOPHIA
Ha! What's that?

CORISCA
The fool has got a sowgelder's horn. [Aside] A post,
As I take it, madam.

SOPHIA
It makes this way still;
Nearer and nearer.

CORISCA
From the camp, I hope.

[Enter **ONE** disguised as a Courier, with a horn; followed by **HILARIO**, in antic armour, with long white hair and beard.

SOPHIA
The messenger appears, and in strange armour.
Heaven! if it be thy will

HILARIO
It is no boot
To strive; our horses tired, let's walk on foot:
And that the castle, which is very near us,
To give us entertainment, may soon hear us,
Blow lustily, my lad, and drawing nigh-a,
Ask for a lady which is cleped Sophia.

CORISCA
He names you, madam.

HILARIO
For to her I bring,
Thus clad in arms, news of a pretty thing,
By name Mathias.

[Exit **COURIER**.

SOPHIA
From my lord? O sir,
I am Sophia, that Mathias' wife.
So may Mars favour you in all your battles,
As you with speed unload me of the burthen
I labour under, till I am confirm 'd

Both where and how you left him!

HILARIO
If thou art,
As I believe, the pigsney of his heart,
Know he's in health, and what's more, full of glee;
And so much I was will'd to say to thee.

SOPHIA
Have you no letters from him?

HILARIO
No more words.
In the camp we use no pens, but write with swords:

Yet, as I am enjoin'd, by word of mouth
I will proclaim his deeds'from north to south;
But tremble not, while I relate the wonder,
Though my eyes like lightning shine, and my voice thunder.

SOPHIA
This is some counterfeit braggart.

CORISCA
Hear him, madam.

HILARIO
The rear march 'd first, which follow'd by the van,
And wing'd with the battalia, no man
Durst stay to shift a shirt, or louse himself;
Yet, ere the armies join'd, that hopeful elf,
Thy dear, thy dainty duckling, bold Mathias,
Advanced, and stared like Hercules or Golias.
A hundred thousand Turks, it is no vaunt,
Assail'd him; every one a Termagaunt:
But what did he, then! with his keen-edge spear
He cut and carbonaded them: here and there
Lay legs and arms; and, as 'tis said trulee
Of Bevis, some he quarter 'd all in three.

SOPHIA
This is ridiculous.

HILARIO
I must take breath;
Then, like a nightingale, I'll sing his death.

SOPHIA

His death!

HILARIO [Aside to **CORISCA**]
I am out.

CORISCA
Recover, dunder-head.

HILARIO
How he escaped, I should have sung, not died;
For, though a knight, when I said so, Hied.
Weary he was, and scarce could stand upright,
And looking round for some courageous knight
To rescue him, as one perplex'd in woe,
He call'd to me, Help, help, Hilario!
My valiant servant, help!

CORISCA
He has spoil'd all.

SOPHIA
Are you the man of arms, then?
I'll make bold
To take off your martial beard, you had fool's hair
Enough without it. Slave! how durst thou make
Thy sport of what concerns me more than life,
In such an antic fashion? Am I grown
Contemptible to those I feed? you, minion,
Had a hand in it too, as it appears;
Your petticoat serves for bases to this warrior.

CORISCA
We did it for your mirth.

HILARIO
For myself, I hope,
I have spoke like a soldier.

SOPHIA
Hence, you rascal!
I never but with reverence name my lord,
And can I hear it by thy tongue profaned,
And not correct thy folly? but you are
Transform'd, and turn'd knight-errant take your course,
And wander where you please; for here I vow
By my lord's life, (an oath I will not break,)
Till his return, or certainty of his safety,
My doors are shut against thee.

[Exit.

CORISCA
You have made
A fine piece of work on't! How do you like the quality?
You had a foolish itch to be an actor,
And may stroll where you please.

HILARIO
Will you buy my share?

CORISCA
No, certainly; I fear I have already
Too much of mine own: I'll only, as a damsel,
(As the books say,) thus far help to disarm you;
And so, dear Don Quixote, taking my leave,
I leave you to your fortune.

[Exit.

HILARIO
Have I sweat
My brains out for this quaint and rare invention,
And am I thus rewarded? I could turn
Tragedian, and roar now, but that I fear
'Twould get me too great a stomach, having no meat
To pacify colon: What will become of me?
I cannot beg in armour, and steal I dare not:
My end must be to stand in a corn field,
And fright away the crows, for bread and cheese;
Or find some hollow tree in the highway,
And there, until my lord return, sell switches:
No more Hilario, but Dolorio now,
I'll weep my eyes out, and be blind of purpose
To move compassion; and so I vanish.

[Exit.

SCENE II. Alba Regalis. An Ante-Room in the Palace

Enter **EUBULUS, UBALDO, RICARDO,** and **OTHERS.**

EUBULUS
Are the gentlemen sent before, as it was order'd
By the king's direction, to entertain

The general?

RICARDO
Long since; they by this have met him,
And given him the bienvenu.

EUBULUS
I hope I need not
Instruct you in your parts.

UBALDO
How! us, my lord!
Fear not; we know our distances and degrees
To the very inch where we are to salute him.

RICARDO
The state were miserable, if the court had none
Of her own breed, familiar with all garbs
Gracious in England, Italy, Spain, or France;
With form and punctuality to receive
Stranger ambassadors: for the general,
He's a mere native, and it matters not
Which way we do accost him.

UBALDO
'Tis great pity
That such as sit at the helm provide no better
For the training up of the gentry. In my judgment
An academy erected, with large pensions
To such as in a table could set down
The congees, cringes, postures, methods, phrase,
Proper to every nation

RICARDO
O, it were
An admirable piece of work!

UBALDO
And yet rich fools
Throw away their charity on hospitals
For beggars and lame soldiers, and ne'er study
The due regard to compliment and courtship,
Matters of more import; and are indeed
The glories of a monarchy!

EUBULUS
These, no doubt,
Are state points, gallants, I confess; but, sure,

Our court needs no aids this way, since it is
A school of nothing else. There are some of you
Whom I forbear to name, whose coining heads
Are the mints of all new fashions, that have done
More hurt to the kingdom by superfluous bravery,
Which the foolish gentry imitate, than a war,
Or a long famine; all the treasure, by
This foul excess, is got into the merchant,
Embroiderer, silk man, jeweller, tailor's hand,
And the third part of the land too, the nobility
Engrossing titles only.

RICARDO
My lord, you are bitter.

[A trumpet.

[Enter a **SERVANT**.

SERVANT
The general is alighted, and now enter'd.

RICARDO
Were he ten generals, I am prepared,
And know what I will do.

EUBULUS
Pray you what, Ricardo?

RICARDO
I'll fight at compliment with him.

UBALDO
I'll charge home too.

EUBULUS
And that's a desperate service; if you come off well.

[Enter **FERDINAND**, **MATHIAS**, **BAPTISTA**, and **CAPTAINS**.

FERDINAND
Captain, command the officers to keep
The soldier, as he march 'd, in rank and file,
Till they hear further from me.

[Exeunt **CAPTAINS**.

EUBULUS

Here's one speaks
In another key; this is no canting language
Taught in your academy.

FERDINAND
Nay, I will present you
To the king myself.

MATHIAS
A grace beyond my merit.

FERDINAND
You undervalue what I cannot set
Too high a price on.

EUBULUS
With a friend's true heart,
I gratulate your return.

FERDINAND
Next to the favour
Of the great king, I am happy in your friendship.

UBALDO
By courtship, coarse on both sides!

FERDINAND
Pray you, receive
This stranger to your knowledge; on my credit,
At all parts he deserves it.

EUBULUS
Your report
Is a strong assurance to me. Sir, most welcome.

MATHIAS
This said by you, the reverence of your age
Commands me to believe it.

RICARDO
This was pretty;
But second me now. I cannot stoop too low
To do your excellence that due observance
Your fortune claims.

EUBULUS
He ne'er thinks on his virtue!

RICARDO
For being, as you are, the soul of soldiers,
And bulwark of Bellona

UBALDO
The protection
Both of the court and king

RICARDO
And the sole minion
Of mighty Mars

UBALDO
One that with justice may
Increase the number of the worthies

EUBULUS
Heyday!

RICARDO
It being impossible in my arms to circle
Such giant worth

UBALDO
At distance we presume
To kiss your honour 'd gauntlet.

EUBULUS
What reply now
Can he make to this foppery?

FERDINAND
You have said,
Gallants, so much, and hitherto done so little,
That, till I learn to speak, and you to do,
I must take time to thank you.

EUBULUS
As I live,
Answer'd as I could wish. How the fops gape now!

RICARDO
This was harsh and scurvy.

UBALDO
We will be revenged
When he comes to court the ladies, and laugh at him.

EUBULUS
Nay, do your offices gentlemen, and conduct
The general to the presence.

RICARDO
Keep your order.

UBALDO
Make way for the general.

[Exeunt all but **EUBULUS**.

EUBULUS
What wise man,
That, with judicious eyes, looks on a soldier,
But must confess that fortune's swing is more
O'er that profession, than all kinds else
Of life pursued by man? They, in a state,
Are but as surgeons to wounded men,
E'en desperate in their hopes: While pain and anguish
Make them blaspheme, and call in vain for death,
Their wives and children kiss the surgeon's knees,
Promise him mountains, if his saving hand
Restore the tortured wretch to former strength:
But when grim death, by Æsculapius' art,
Is frighted from the house, and health appears
In sanguine colours on the sick man's face,
All is forgot; and, asking his reward,
He's paid with curses, often receives wounds
From him whose wounds he cured: so soldiers,
Though of more worth and use, meet the same fate,
As it is too apparent. I have observ'd,
When horrid Mars, the touch of whose rough hand
With palsies shakes a kingdom, hath put on
His dreadful helmet, and with terror fills
The place where he, like an unwelcome guest.
Resolves to revel, how the lords of her, like
The tradesman, merchant, and litigious pleader,
And such like scarabs bred in the dung of peace,
In hope of their protection, humbly offer
Their daughters to their beds, heirs to their sen-ice,
And wash with tears their sweat, their dust, their scars:
But when those clouds of war, that menaced
A bloody deluge to the affrighted state,
Are, by their breath, dispersed, and overblown,
And famine, blood, and death, Bellona's pages,
Whipt from the quiet continent to Thrace;
Soldiers, that, like the foolish hedge-sparrow,

To their own ruin, hatch this cuckoo, peace,
Are straight thought burthensome; since want of means,
Growing from want of action, breeds contempt:
And that, the worst of ills, falls to their lot,
Their service, with the danger, soon forgot.

[Enter a **SERVANT**.

SERVANT
The queen, my lord, hath made choice of this room,
To see the masque.

EUBULUS
I'll be a looker on:
My dancing days are past.

[Loud music.

[Enter **UBALDO, RICARDO, LADISLAUS, FERDINAND, HONORIA, MATHIAS, SYLVIA, ACANTHE, BAPTISTA, CAPTAINS,** and **OTHERS**. As they pass, a Song in praise of war.

LADISLAUS
This courtesy
To a stranger, my Honoria, keeps fair rank
With all your rarities. After your travail,
Look on our court delights; but first, from your
Relation, with erected ears, I'll hear
The music of your war, which must be sweet,
Ending in victory.

FERDINAND
Not to trouble
Your majesties with description of a battle
Too full of horror for the place, and to
Avoid particulars, which should I deliver,
I must trench longer on your patience, than
My manners will give way to; in a word, sir,
It was well fought on both sides, and almost
With equal fortune, it continuing doubtful
Upon whose tents plumed Victory would take
Her glorious stand. Impatient of delay,
With the flower of our prime gentlemen, I charged
Their main battalia, and with their assistance
Brake in; but, when I was almost assured
That they were routed, by a stratagem
Of the subtile Turk, who opened his gross body,
And rallied up his troops on either side,
I found myself so far engaged, for I

Must not conceal my errors, that I knew not
Which way with honour to come off.

EUBULUS
Like
A general that tells his faults, and is not
Ambitious to engross unto himself
All honour, as some have, in which, with justice,
They could not claim a share.

FERDINAND
Being thus hemm'd in,
Their scimitars raged among us; and, my horse
Kill'd under me, I every minute looked for
An honourable end, and that was all
My hope could fashion to me: circled thus
With death and horror, as one sent from heaven,
This man of men, with some choice horse, that follow'd
His brave example, did pursue the track
His sword cut for them, and, but that I see him
Already blush to hear what he, being present,
I know would wish unspoken, I should say, sir,
By what he did, we boldly may believe
All that is writ of Hector.

MATHIAS
General,
Pray spare these strange hyperboles.

EUBULUS
Do not blush
To hear a truth; here are a pair of monsieurs,
Had they been in your place, would have run away,
And ne'er changed countenance.

UBALDO
We have your good word still.

EUBULUS
And shall, while you deserve it.

LADISLAUS
Silence; on.

FERDINAND
He, as I said, like dreadful lightning thrown
From Jupiter's shield, dispersed the armed gire
With which I was environed; horse and man

Shrunk under his strong arm: more, with his looks
Frighted, the valiant fled, with which encouraged,
My soldiers, (like young eaglets preying under
The wings of their fierce dam,) as if from him
They took both spirit and fire, bravely came on.
By him I was remounted, and inspired
With treble courage; and such as fled before
Boldly made head again; and, to confirm them,
It suddenly was apparent, that the fortune
Of the day was ours; each soldier and commander
Perform'd his part; but this was the great wheel
By which the lesser moved: and all rewards
And signs of honour, as the civic garland,
The mural wreath, the enemy's prime horse,
With the general's sword, and armour, (the old honours
With which the Romans crown'd their several leaders,)
To him alone are proper.

LADISLAUS
And they shall
Deservedly fall on him. Sit; 'tis our pleasure.

FERDINAND
Which I must serve, not argue.

HONORIA
You are a stranger,
But, in your service for the king, a native.
And, though a free queen, I am bound in duty.
To cherish virtue wheresoe'er I find it:
This place is yours.

MATHIAS
It were presumption in me
To sit so near you.

HONORIA
Not, having our warrant.

[Music within.

LADISLAUS
Let the masquers enter: by the preparation,
'Tis a French brawl, an apish imitation
Of what you really perform in battle:
And Pallas, bound up in a little volume,
Apollo, with his lute, attending on her,
Serve for the induction.

[Enter **MASQUERS**, &c. **PALLAS**, accompanied by **APOLLO** on the lute.

Though we contemplate to express
The glory of your happiness,
That, by your powerful arm, have been
So true a victor, that no sin
Could ever taint you with a blame
To lessen your deserved fame.
Or, though we contend to set
Your worth in the full height, or get
Celestial singers crown d with bays,
With flourishes to dress your praise:
You know your conquest; but your story
Lives in your triumphant glory.

[A Dance.

LADISLAUS
Our thanks to all.
To the banquet that's prepared to entertain them:

[Exeunt **MASQUERS**, **APOLLO**, and **PALLAS**.

What would my best Honoria?

HONORIA
May it please
My king, that I, who, by his suffrage, ever
Have had power to command, may now entreat
An honour from him.

LADISLAUS
Why should you desire
What is your own? whate'er it be, you are
The mistress of it.

HONORIA
I am happy in
Your grant: my suit, sir, is, that your commanders,
Especially this stranger, may, as I,
In my discretion, shall think good, receive
What's due to their deserts.

LADISLAUS
What you determine
Shall know no alteration.

EUBULUS

The soldier
Is like to have good usage, when he depends
Upon her pleasure! Are all the men so bad,
That, to give satisfaction, we must have
A woman treasurer? Heaven help all!

HONORIA

With you, sir, [To **MATHIAS**]
I will begin, and, as in my esteem
You are most eminent, expect to have
What's fit for me to give, and you to take.
The favour in the quick dispatch being double,
Go fetch my casket, and with speed.

[Exit **ACANTHE**.

EUBULUS

The kingdom
Is very bare of money, when rewards
Issue from the queen's jewel-house. Give him gold
And store, no question the gentleman wants it.
Good madam, what shall he do with a hoop ring,
And a spark of diamond in it? though you take it,

[Re-enter **ACANTHE** with a Casket.

For the greater honour, from your majesty's finger,
'Twill not increase the value. He must purchase
Rich suits, the gay caparison of courtship,
Revel and feast, which, the war ended, is
A soldier's glory; and 'tis fit that way
Your bounty should provide for him.

HONORIA

You are rude,
And by your narrow thoughts proportion mine.
What I will do now shall be worth the envy
Of Cleopatra. Open it; see here

[**HONORIA** descends from the state.

The lapidary's idol! Gold is trash,
And a poor salary fit for grooms; wear these,
As studded stars in your armour, and make the sun
Look dim with jealousy of a greater light
Than his beams gild the day with: when it is
Exposed to view, call it Honoria's gift,

The queen Honoria's gift, that loves a soldier;
And, to give ornament and lustre to him,
Parts freely with her own! Yet, not to take
From the magnificence of the king, I will
Dispense his bounty too, but as a page
To wait on mine; for other tosses, take
A hundred thousand crowns: your hand, dear sir

[Takes off the king's signet.

And this shall be thy warrant.

EUBULUS
I perceive
I was cheated in this woman: now she is
In the giving vein to soldiers, let her be proud,
And the king dote, so she go on, I care not.

HONORIA
This done, our pleasure is, that all arrearages
Be paid unto the captains, and their troops;
With a large donative, to increase their zeal
For the service of the kingdom.

EUBULUS
Better still:
Let men of arms be used thus, if they do not
Charge desperately upon the cannon's mouth,
Though the devil roar'd, and fight like dragons, hang me!
Now they may drink sack: but small beer, with a passport
To beg with as they travel, and no money,
Turns their red blood to buttermilk.

HONORIA
Are you pleased, sir,
With what I have done?

LADISLAUS
Yes, and thus confirm it,
With this addition of mine own: You have, sir,
From our loved queen received some recompense
For your life hazarded in the late action;
And, that we may follow her great example
In cherishing valour, without limit ask
What you from us can wish.

MATHIAS
If it be true,

Dread sir, as 'tis affirm'd, that every soil,
Where he is well, is to a valiant man
His natural country, reason may assure me
I should fix here, where blessings beyond hope,
From you, the spring, like rivers, flow unto me.
If wealth were my ambition, by the queen
I am made rich already, to the amazement
Of all that see, or shall hereafter read
The story of her bounty; if to spend
The remnant of my life in deeds of arms,
No region is more fertile of good knights,
From whom my knowledge that way may be better'd
Than this your warlike Hungary; if favour,
Or grace in court could take me, by your grant,
Far, far, beyond my merit, I may make
In yours a free election; but, alas! sir,
I am not mine own, but by my destiny
(Which I cannot resist) forced to prefer
My country's smoke, before the glorious fire
With which your bounties warm me. All I ask, sir,
By amorous letters, vows made for her service,
With all the engines wanton appetite
Could mount to shake the fortress of her honour,
Here, here is my assurance she holds out,

[Kisses the picture.

And is impregnable.

HONORIA
What's that?

MATHIAS
Her fair figure.

LADISLAUS
As I live, an excellent face!

HONORIA
You have seen a better.

LADISLAUS
I ever except yours: nay, frown not, sweetest,
The Cyprian queen, compared to you, in my
Opinion, is a negro. As you order'd,
I'll see the soldiers paid; and, in my absence,
Pray you use your powerful arguments, to stay
This gentleman in our service.

Though I cannot be ignorant it must relish
Of foul ingratitude, is your gracious license
For my departure.

LADISLAUS
Whither?

MATHIAS
To my own home, sir,
My own poor home; which will, at my return,
Grow rich by your magnificence. I am here
But a body without a soul; and, till I find it
In the embraces of my constant wife,
And, to set off that constancy, in her beauty
And matchless excellences, without a rival,
I am but half myself.

HONORIA
And is she then
So chaste and fair as you infer?

MATHIAS
O, madam,
Though it must argue weakness in a rich man,
To shew his gold before an armed thief,
And I, in praising of my wife, but feed
The fire of lust in others to attempt her;
Such is my full-sail 'd confidence in her virtue,

LADISLAUS
On to the camp.

[Exeunt **LADISLAUS, FERDINAND, EUBULUS, BAPTISTA,** and **OFFICERS.**

HONORIA
I am full of thoughts,
And something there is here I must give form to,
Though yet an embryon: [Aside] You, signiors,
Have no business with the soldier, as I ake it,
Though in my absence she were now besieged
By a strong army of lascivious wooers,
And every one more expert in his art,
Than those that tempted chaste Penelope;
You are for other warfare; quit the place,
But be within call.

RICARDO
Employment, on my life, boy!

UBALDO
If it lie in our road, we are made for ever.

[Exeunt **UBALDO** and **RICARDO**.

HONORIA
You may perceive the king is no way tainted
With the disease of jealousy, since he leaves me
Thus private with you.

MATHIAS
It were in him, madam,
A sin unpardonable to distrust such pureness,
Though I were an Adonis.

HONORIA
I presume
He neither does nor dares: and yet the story
Delivered of you by the general,
With your heroic courage, which sinks deeply
Into a knowing woman's heart, besides
Your promising presence, might beget some scruple
In a meaner man; but more of this hereafter.
Though they raised batteries by prodigal gifts,
I'll take another theme now, and conjure you
By the honours you have won, and by the love
Sacred to your dear wife, to answer truly
To what I shall demand.

MATHIAS
You need not use
Charms to this purpose, madam.

HONORIA
Tell me, then,
Being yourself assured 'tis not in man
To sully with one spot th' immaculate whiteness
Of your wife's honour, if you have not, since
The Gordian of your love was tied by marriage,
Play'd false with her?

MATHIAS
By the hopes of mercy, never.

HONORIA
It may be, not frequenting the converse
Of handsome ladies, you were never tempted,

And so your faith's untried yet.

MATHIAS
Surely, madam,
I am no woman-hater; I have been
Received to the society of the best
And fairest of our climate, and have met with
No common entertainment, yet ne'er felt
The least heat that way.

HONORIA
Strange! and do you think still,
The earth can show no beauty that can drench
In Lethe all remembrance of the favour
You now bear to your own?

MATHIAS
Nature must find out
Some other mould to fashion a new creature
Fairer than her Pandora, ere I prove
Guilty, or in my wishes or my thoughts,
To my Sophia.

HONORIA
Sir, consider better;
Not one in our whole sex?

MATHIAS
I am constant to
My resolution.

HONORIA
But dare you stand
The opposition, and bind yourself
By oath for the performance?

MATHIAS
My faith else
Had but a weak foundation.

HONORIA
I take hold
Upon your promise, and enjoin your stay
For one month here.

MATHIAS
I am caught! [Aside.

HONORIA

And if I do not
Produce a lady, in that time, that shall
Make you confess your error, I submit
Myself to any penalty you shall please
To impose upon me: in the mean space, write
To your chaste wife, acquaint her with your fortune:
The jewels that were mine you may send to her,
For better confirmation. I'll provide you
Of trusty messengers: but how far distant is she?

MATHIAS

A day's hard riding.

HONORIA

There is no retiring;
I'LL bind you to your word.

MATHIAS

Well, since there is
No way to shun it, I will stand the hazard,
And instantly make ready my dispatch:
Till then, I'll leave your majesty.

[Exit.

HONORIA

How I burst
With envy, that there lives, besides myself,
One fair and loyal woman! 'twas the end
Of my ambition to be recorded
The only wonder of the age, and shall I
Give way to a competitor? Nay more,
To add to my affliction, the assurances
That I placed in my beauty have deceived me:
I thought one amorous glance of mine could bring
All hearts to my subjection; but this stranger,
Unmoved as rocks, contemns me. But I cannot
Sit down so with mine honour: I will gain
A double victory, by working him
To my desire, and taint her in her honour,
Or lose myself: I have read that sometime poison
Is useful. To supplant her, I'll employ,
With any cost, Ubaldo and Ricardo,
Two noted courtiers, of approved cunning
In all the windings of lust's labyrinth;
And in corrupting him, I will outgo
Nero's Poppaea: if he shut his ears

Against my Syren notes, I'll boldly swear,
Ulysses lives again; or that I have found
A frozen cynic, cold in spite of all
Allurements; one whom beauty cannot move,.
Nor softest blandishments entice to love.

[Exit.

SCENE I. Bohemia. A Space near the Entrance of Mathias' House

Enter **HILARIO**, with a pitcher of water, and a wallet.

HILARIO
Thin, thin provision! I am dieted
Like one set to watch hawks; and, to keep me waking,
My croaking guts make a perpetual larum.
Here I stand centinel; and, though I fright
Beggars from my lady's gate, in hope to have
A greater share, I find my commons mend not.
I look'd this morning in my glass, the river,
And there appear'd a fish call'd a poor John,
Cut with a lenten face, in my own likeness;
And it seem'd to speak, and say, Good morrow, cousin!
No man comes this way but has a fling at me:
A surgeon passing by, ask'd at what rate
I would sell myself; I answered, For what.
To make, said he, a living anatomy,
And set thee up in our hall, for thou art transparent
Without dissection; and, indeed, he had reason:
For I am scour'd with this poor purge to nothing.
They say that hunger dwells in the camp; but till
My lord returns, or certain tidings of him,
He will not part with me: but sorrow's dry,
And I must drink howsoever.

[Enter **UBALDO, RICARDO** and a **GUIDE**.

GUIDE
That's her castle,
Upon my certain knowledge.

UBALDO
Our horses held out
To my desire. I am afire to be at it.

RICARDO
Take the jades for thy reward; before I part hence,
I hope to be better carried. Give me the cabinet:
So; leave us now.

GUIDE
Good fortune to you, gallants!

[Exit.

UBALDO
Being joint agents, in a design of trust too,
For the service of the queen, and our own pleasure,
Let us proceed with judgment.

RICARDO
If I take not
This fort at the first assault, make me an eunuch;
So I may have precedence,

UBALDO
On no terms.
We are both to play one prize; he that works best
In the searching of this mine, shall carry it,
Without contention.

RICARDO
Make you your approaches
As I directed.

UBALDO
I need no instruction;
I work not on your anvil. I'll give fire
With mine own linstock; if the powder be dank,
The devil rend the touch-hole! Who have we here?
What skeleton's this?

RICARDO
A ghost! or the image ot famine!
Where dost thou dwell?

HILARIO
Dwell, sir! my dwelling is
In the highway: that goodly house was once
My habitation, but I am banish 'd,
And cannot be call'd home till news arrive
Of the good knight Mathias.

RICARDO
If that will
Restore thee, thou art safe.

UBALDO
We come from him,
With presents to his lady.

HILARIO
But are you sure
He is in health?

RICARDO
Never so well: conduct us
To the lady.

HILARIO
Though a poor snake, I will leap
Out of my skin for joy. Break, pitcher, break!
And wallet, late my cupboard, I bequeath thee
To the next beggar; thou, red herring, swim
To the Red Sea again: methinks I am already
Knuckle deep in the fieshpots; and, though waking, dream
Of wine and plenty!

RICARDO
What's the mystery
Of this strange passion?

HILARIO
My belly, gentlemen,
Will not give me leave to tell you; when I have brought you
To my lady's presence, I am disenchanted:
There you shall know all. Follow; if I outstrip you,
Know I run for my belly.

UBALDO
A mad fellow.

[Exeunt.

SCENE II. A Room in Mathias' House

Enter **SOPHIA** and **CORISCA**.

SOPHIA
Do not again delude me.

CORISCA
If I do,
Send me a grazing with my fellow, Hilario.
I stood as you commanded, in the turret,
Observing all that pass'd by; and even now,
I did discern a pair of cavaliers,
For such their outside spoke them, with their guide,
Dismounting from their horses; they said something
To our hungry centinel, that made him caper
And frisk in the air for joy: and, to confirm this,
See, madam, they're in view.

[Enter **HILARIO**, **UBALDO**, and **RICARDO**.

HILARIO
News from my lord!
Tidings of joy! these are no counterfeits,
But knights indeed. Dear madam, sign my pardon,
That I may feed again, and pick up my crumbs;
I have had a long fast of it.

SOPHIA
Eat, I forgive thee.

HILARIO
O comfortable words! Eat, I forgive thee!
And if in this I do not soon obey you,
And ram in to the purpose, billet me again
In the highway. Butler and cook, be ready,
For I enter like a tyrant.

[Exit.

UBALDO
Since mine eyes
Were never happy in so sweet an object,
Without inquiry, I presume you are
The lady of the house, and so salute you.

RICARDO
This letter, with these jewels, from your lord,
Warrant my boldness, madam.

[Delivers a letter and a casket.

UBALDO
In being a sen-ant
To such rare beauty, you must needs deserve
This courtesy from a stranger.

[Salutes **CORISCA**.

RICARDO
You are still
Beforehand with me. Pretty one, I descend
To take the height of your lip; and, if I miss
In the altitude, hereafter, if you please,
I will make use of my Jacob's staff.

[Salutes **CORISCA**.

CORISCA
These gentlemen
Have certainly had good breeding, as it appears
By their neat kissing, they hit me so pat on the lips,
At the first sight.

[In the interim, **SOPHIA** reads the letter, and opens the casket.

SOPHIA
Heaven, in thy mercy, make me
Thy thankful handmaid for this boundless blessing,
In thy goodness shower'd upon me!

UBALDO
I do not like
This simple devotion in her; it is seldom
Practised among my mistresses.

RICARDO
Or mine.
Would they kneel to I know not who, for the possession
Of such inestimable wealth, before
They thank'd the bringers of it? the poor lady
Does want instruction, but I'll be her tutor,
And read her another lesson.

SOPHIA
If I have
Shewn want of manners, gentlemen, in my slowness
To pay the thanks I owe you for your travail,
To do my lord and me, howe'er unworthy
Of such a benefit, this noble favour,

Impute it, in your clemency, to the excess
Of joy that overwhelm'd me.

RICARDO
She speaks well.

UBALDO
Polite and courtly.

SOPHIA
And howe'er it may
Increase the offence, to trouble you with more
Demands touching my lord, before I have
Invited you to taste such as the coarseness
Of my poor house can offer; pray you connive
On my weak tenderness, though I entreat
To learn from you something he hath, it may be,
In his letter left unmention'd.

RICARDO
I can only
Give you assurance that he is in health,
Graced by the king and queen.

UBALDO
And in the court
With admiration look'd on.

RICARDO
You must therefore
Put off these widow's garments, and appear
Like to yourself.

UBALDO
And entertain all pleasures
Your fortune marks out for you.

RICARDO
There are other
Particular privacies, which on occasion
I will deliver to you.

SOPHIA
You oblige me
To your service ever.

RICARDO
Good! your service; mark that.

SOPHIA
In the mean time, by your good acceptance make
My rustic entertainment relish of
The curiousness of the court.

UBALDO
Your looks, sweet madam,
Cannot but make each dish a feast.

SOPHIA
It shall be
Such, in the freedom of my will to please you.
I'll shew you the way: this is too great an honour,

From such brave guests, to me so mean an hostess.

[Exeunt.

SCENE III. Alba Regalis. An Outer-room in the Palace

Enter **ACANTHE**, and four or five **SERVANTS** with visors.

ACANTHE
You know your charge; give it action, and expect
Rewards beyond your hopes.

1ST SERVANT
If we but eye them,
They are ours, I warrant you.

2ND SERVANT
May we not ask why
We are put upon this?

ACANTHE
Let that stop your mouth;

[Gives them money.

And learn more manners, groom. 'Tis upon the hour
In which they use to walk here: when you have them
In your power, with violence carry them to the place
Where I appointed; there I will expect you:
Be bold and careful.

[Exit.

[Enter **MATHIAS** and **BAPTISTA**.

1ST SERVANT
These are they.

2ND SERVANT
Are you sure?

1ST SERVANT
Am I sure I am myself?

2ND SERVANT
Seize on him strongly; if he have but means
To draw his sword, 'tis ten to one we smart for't:
Take all advantages.

MATHIAS
I cannot guess
What her intents are; but her carriage was
As I but now related.

BAPTISTA
Your assurance
In the constancy of your lady is the armour
That must defend you. Where's the picture?

MATHIAS
Here,
And no way alter 'd.

BAPTISTA
If she be not perfect,
There is no truth in art.

MATHIAS
By this, I hope,
She hath received my letters.

BAPTISTA
Without question:
These courtiers are rank riders, when they are
To visit a handsome lady.

MATHIAS
Lend me your ear.
One piece of her entertainment will require

Your dearest privacy.

1ST SERVANT
Now they stand fair;
Upon them.

[They rush forward.

MATHIAS
Villains!

1ST SERVANT
Stop their mouths. We come not
To try your valours: kill him, if he offer
To ope his mouth. We have you: 'tis in vain
To make resistance. Mount them, and away.

[Exeunt with **MATHIAS** and **BAPTISTA**.

SCENE IV. A Gallery in the Same

Enter **SERVANTS** with lights, **LADISLAUS**, **FERDINAND**, and **EUBULUS**.

LADISLAUS
'Tis late. Go to your rest; but do not envy
The happiness I draw near to.

EUBULUS
If you enjoy it
The moderate way, the sport yields, I confess,
A pretty titillation; but too much oft
Will bring you on your knees. In my younger days
I was myself a gamester; and I found
By sad experience, there is no such soaker
As ayoung spongy wife; she keeps a thousand
Horse-leeches in her box, and the thieves will suck out
Both blood and marrow! I feel a kind of cramp
In my joints, when I think on't: but it may be queens,
And such a queen as yours is has the art

FERDINAND
You take leave
To talk, my lord.

LADISLAUS
He may, since he can do nothing.

EUBULUS
If you spend this way too much of your royal stock,
Ere long we may be puefellows.

LADISLAUS
The door shut!
Knock gently; harder. So, here comes her woman.
Take off my gown.

[Enter **ACANTHE**.

ACANTHE
My lord, the queen by me
This night desires your pardon.

LADISLAUS
How, Acanthe!
I come by her appointment; 'twas her grant;
The motion was her own.

ACANTHE
It may be, sir;
But by her doctors she is since advised,
For her health's sake, to forbear,

EUBULUS
I do not like
This physical letchery, the old downright way
Is worth a thousand on't.

LADISLAUS
Prithee, Acanthe,
Mediate for me.

[Offering her a ring.

EUBULUS
O the fiends of hell!
Would any man bribe his servant, to make way
To his own wife? if this be the court state,
Shame fall on such as use it!

ACANTHE
By this jewel,
This night I dare not move her, but tomorrow
I will watch all occasions.

LADISLAUS
Take this,
To be mindful of me.

EUBULUS
'Slight, I thought a king
Might have ta'en up any woman at the king's price;
And must he buy his own, at a dearer rate
Than a stranger in a brothel?

LADISLAUS
What is that
You mutter, sir?

EUBULUS
No treason to your honour:
I'll speak it out, though it anger you; if you; pay for
Your lawful pleasure in some kind, great sir,
What do you make the queen? cannot you clicket
Without a fee, or when she has a suit
For you to grant?

[**LADISLAUS** draws his sword.

FERDINAND
O hold, sir!

LADISLAUS
Off with his head!

EUBULUS
Do, when you please; you but blow out a taper
That would light your understanding, and, in care oft,
Is burnt down to the socket. Be as you are, sir,
An absolute monarch: it did shew more king-like
In those libidinous Caesars, that compell'd
Matrons and virgins of all ranks to bow
Unto their ravenous lusts; and did admit
Of more excuse than I can urge for you,
That slave yourself to the imperious humour
Of a proud beauty.

LADISLAUS
Out of my sight!

EUBULUS
I will, sir,
Give way to your furious passion; but when reason

Hath got the better of it, I much hope
The counsel that offends now will deserve
Your royal thanks. Tranquillity of mind
Stay with you, sir! I do begin to doubt
There's something more in the queen's strangeness than
Is yet disclosed; and I will find it out,
Or lose myself in the search.

[Aside, and exit.

FERDINAND
Sure he is honest,
And from your infancy hath truly served you:
Let that plead for him; and impute this harshness
To the frowardness of his age.

LADISLAUS
I am much troubled,
And do begin to stagger. Ferdinand, good night!
To-morrow visit us. Back to our own lodgings.

[Exeunt.

SCENE V. Another Room in the Same

Enter **ACANTHE** and the visored **SERVANTS**, with **MATHIAS** and **BAPTISTA** blindfolded.

ACANTHE
You have done bravely. Lock this in that room,
There let him ruminate; I'll anon unhood him:

[They carry off **BAPTISTA**.

The other must stay here. As soon as I
Have quit the place, give him the liberty
And use of his eyes; that done, disperse yourselves
As privately as you can: but, on your lives,
No word of what hath pass'd.

[Exit.

1ST SERVANT
If I do, sell
My tongue to a tripe-wife. Come, unbind his arms:
You are now at your own disposure; and however
We used you roughly, I hope you will find here

Such entertainment as will give you cause
To thank us for the service: and so I leave you.

[Exeunt **SERVANTS**.

MATHIAS
If I am in a prison, 'tis a neat one.
What Œdipus can resolve this riddle? Ha!
I never gave just cause to any man
Basely to plot against my life: But what is
Become of my true friend? for him I suffer
More than myself.

ACANTHE [within]
Remove that idle fear;
He's safe as you are.

MATHIAS
Whosoe'er thou art,
For him I thank thee. I cannot imagine
Where I should be: though I have read the tales
Of errant-knighthood, stuff d with the relations
Of magical enchantments; yet I am not
So sottishly credulous to believe the devil
Hath that way power.

[Music above.

Ha! music?
The blushing rose, and purple flower,
Let grow too long, are soonest blasted;
Dainty fruits, though sweet, will sour,
And rot in ripeness, left untasted.
Yet here is one more sweet than these:
The more you taste the more she' ll please.
Beauty that's enclosed with ice,
Is a shadow chaste as rare;
Then how much those sweets entice,
That have issue full as fair!
Earth cannot yield, from all her powers,
One equal for dame Venus' bowers.
A song too! certainly, be it he or she
That owes this voice, it hath not been acquainted
With much affliction. Whosoe'er you are
That do inhabit here, if you have bodies,
And are not mere aerial forms, appear,

[Enter **HONORIA** masked.

And make me know your end with me.
Most strange!
What have I conjured up? sure, if this be
A spirit, it is no damn'd one. What a shape's here!
Then, with what majesty it moves! If Juno
Were now to keep her state among the gods,
And Hercules to be made again her guest,
She could not put on a more glorious habit,
Though her handmaid, Iris, lent her various colours,
Or old Oceanus ravish 'd from the deep
All jewels shipwreck'd in it. As you have
Thus far made known yourself, it that your face
Have not too much divinity about it
For mortal eyes to gaze on, perfect what
You have begun, with wonder and amazement
To my astonish'd senses.

[**HONORIA** unmasks.

How! the queen!

[Kneels.

HONORIA
Rise, sir, and hear my reasons, in defence
Of the rape (for so you may conceive) which I,
By my instruments, made upon you. You, perhaps,
May think what you have suffer 'd for my lust
Is a common practice with me; but I call
Those ever-shining lamas, and their great
Maker,
As witnesses of my innocence: I ne'er look'd on
A man but your best self, on whom I ever
(Except the king) vouchsafed an eye of favour.

MATHIAS
The king, indeed, and only such a king,
Deserves your rarities, madam; and, but he,
'Twere giant-like ambition in any,
In his wishes only, to presume to taste
The nectar of your kisses; or to feed
His appetite with that ambrosia, due
And proper to a prince; and, what binds more,
A lawful husband. For myself, great queen,
I am a thing obscure, disfurnish'd of
All merit, that can raise me higher than,
In my most humble thankfulness for your bounty,

To hazard my life for you; and, that way,
I am most ambitious.

HONORIA
I desire no more
Than what you promise. If you dare expose
Your life, as you profess, to do me service,
How can it be better employ'd than in
Preserving mine? which only you can do,
And must do, with the danger of your own,
A desperate danger too! If private men
Can brook no rivals in what they affect,
But to the death pursue such as invade
What law makes their inheritance; the king,
To whom you know I am dearer than his crown,
His health, his eyes, his after hopes, with all
His present blessings, must fall on that man,
Like dreadful lightning, that is won by prayers,
Threats, or rewards, to stain his bed, or make
His hoped-for issue doubtful!

MATHIAS
If you aim
At what I more than fear you do, the reasons
Which you deliver, should, in judgment, rather
Deter me, than invite a grant, with my
Assured ruin.

HONORIA
True; if that you were
Of a cold temper, one whom doubt, or fear,
In the most horrid forms they could put on,
Might teach to be ingrateful. Your denial
To me, that have deserved so much, is more,
If it can have addition.

MATHIAS
I know not
What your commands are.

HONORIA
Have you fought so well
Among arm'd men, yet cannot guess what lists
You are to enter, when you are in private
With a willing lady: one, that, to enjoy
Your company this night, denied the king
Access to what's his own? If you will press me
To speak in plainer language

MATHIAS

Pray you, forbear;
I would I did not understand too much!
Already, by your words, I am instructed
To credit that, which, not confirm 'd by you,
Had bred suspicion in me of untruth,
Though an angel had affirm 'd it. But suppose
That, cloy'd with happiness, which is ever built
On virtuous chastity, in the wantonness
Of appetite, you desire to make trial
Of the false delights proposed by vicious lust;
Among ten thousand, every way more able
And apter to be wrought on, such as owe you
Obedience, being your subjects, why should you
Make choice of me, a stranger?

HONORIA

Though yet reason
Was ne'er admitted in the court of love,
I'll yield you one unanswerable. As I urged,
In our last private conference, you have
A pretty promising presence; but there are
Many, in limbs and feature, who may take,
That way, the right-hand file of you: besides,
Your May of youth is past, and the blood spent
By wounds, though bravely taken, renders you
Disabled for love's service: and that valour
Set off with better fortune, which, it may be,
Swells you above your bounds, is not the hook
That hath caught me, good sir. I need no champion,
With his sword, to guard my honour or my beauty;
In both I can defend myself, and live
My own protection.

MATHIAS

If these advocates,
The best that can plead for me, have no power,
What can you find in me else, that may tempt you,
With irrecoverable loss unto yourself,
To be a gainer from me?

HONORIA

You have, sir,
A jewel of such matchless worth and lustre,
As does disdain comparison, and darkens
All that is rare in other men; and that,
I must or win or lessen.

MATHIAS

You heap more
Amazement on me: What am I possess 'd of
That you can covet? make me understand it,
If it have a name.

HONORIA

Yes, an imagined one;
But is, in substance, nothing; being a garment
Worn out of fashion, and long since given o'er
By the court and country: 'tis your loyalty
And constancy to your wife; 'tis that I dote on,
And does deserve my envy; and that jewel,
Or by fair play or foul, I must win from you.

MATHIAS

These are mere contraries. If you love me, madam,
For my constancy, why seek you to destroy it?
In my keeping it preserve me worth your favour.
Or, if it be a jewel of that value,
As you with labour'd rhetoric would persuade me,
What can you stake against it?

HONORIA

A queen's fame,
And equal honour.

MATHIAS

So, whoever wins,
Both shall be losers.

HONORIA

That is that I aim at:
Yet on the die I lay rny youth, my beauty,
This moist palm, this soft lip, and those delights
Darkness should only judge of.

[Kisses him.

Do you find them
Infectious in the trial, that you start,
As frighted with their touch?

MATHIAS

Is it in man
To resist such strong temptations?

HONORIA

He begins
To waver. [Aside.

MATHIAS

Madam, as you are gracious,
Grant this short night's deliberation to me;
And, with the rising sun, from me you shall
Receive full satisfaction.

HONORIA

Though extremes
Hate all delay, I will deny you nothing.
This key will bring you to your friend; you are safe both;
And all things useful that could be prepared
For one I love and honour, wait upon you.
Take counsel of your pillow, such a fortune
As with affection's swiftest wings flies to you,
Will not be often tender'd.

[Exit.

MATHIAS

How my blood
Rebels! I now could call her back and yet
There's something stays me: if the king had tender'd
Such favours to my wife, 'tis to be doubted
They had not been refused: but, being a man,
I should not yield first, or prove an example,
For her defence, of frailty. By this, sans question,
She's tempted too; and here I may examine.

[Looks on the picture.

How she holds out. She's still the same, the same
Pure crystal rock of chastity. Perish all
Allurements that may alter me! The snow
Of her sweet -coldness hath extinguish'd quite
The fire that but even now began to flame:
And I by her confirm'd, rewards nor titles.
Nor certain death from the refused queen,
Shall shake my faith; since I resolve to be
Loyal to her, as she is true to me.

[Exit.

Enter **UBALDO** and **RICARDO**.

UBALDO
What we spake on the voley begins to work;
We have laid a good foundation.

RICARDO
Build it up,
Or else 'tis nothing: you have by lot the honour
Of the first assault; but, as it is condition'd,
Observe the time proportion 'd: I'll not part with
My share in the achievement; when I whistle,
Or hem, fall off.

[Enter **SOPHIA**.

UBALDO
She comes. Stand by, I'll watch
My opportunity. [They walk aside.

SOPHIA
I find myself
Strangely distracted with the various stories,
Now well, now ill, then doubtfully, by my guests
Deliver'd of my lord: and, like poor beggars
That in their dreams find treasure, by reflection
Of a wounded fancy, make it questionable
Whether they sleep or not; yet, tickled with
Such a fantastic hope of happiness,
Wish they may never wake. In some such measure,
Incredulous of what I see and touch,
As 'twere a fading apparition, I
Am still perplex'd, and troubled; and when, most
Confirm'd 'tis true, a curious jealousy
To be assured, by what means, and from whom,
Such a mass of wealth was first deserv'd, then gotten,
Cunningly steals into me. I have practised,
For my certain resolution, with these courtiers.
Promising private conference to either,
And, at this hour: if in search of the truth,
I hear, or say, more than becomes my virtue,
Forgive me, my Mathias.

UBALDO
Now I make in.

[Comes forward.

Madam, as you commanded, I attend
Your pleasure.

SOPHIA
I must thank you for the favour.

UBALDO
I am no ghostly father; yet, if you have
Some scruples touching your lord, you would be resolved of,
I am prepared.

SOPHIA
But will you take your oath,
To answer truly?

UBALDO
On the hem of your smock, if you please:
A vow I dare not break, it being a book
I would gladly swear on.

SOPHIA
To spare, sir, that trouble,
I'll take your word, which, in a gentleman,
Should be of equal value. Is my lord, then,
In such grace with the queen?

UBALDO
You should best know,
By what you have found from him, whether he can
Deserve a grace or no.

SOPHIA
What grace clo you mean?

UBALDO
That special grace, if you will have it, he
Labour 'd so hard for between a pair of sheets,
Upon your wedding night, when your ladyship
Lost you know what.

SOPHIA
Fie! be more modest,
Or I must leave you.

UBALDO
I would tell a truth

As cleanly as I could, and yet the subject
Makes me run out a little.

SOPHIA
You would put, now,
A foolish jealousy in my head, my lord
Hath gotten a new mistress.

UBALDO
One! a hundred;
But under seal I speak it: I presume
Upon your silence, it being for your profit.
They talk of Hercules' fifty in a night,
'Twas well; but yet to yours he was a piddler:
Such a soldier and a courtier never came
To Alba Regalis; the ladies run mad for him,
And there is such contention among them,
Who shall engross him wholly, that the like
Was never heard of.

SOPHIA
Are they handsome women?

UBALDO
Fie! no; coarse mammets: and what's worse, they are old too,
Some fifty, some threescore, and they pay dear for't,
Believing that he carries a powder in his breeches
Will make them young again; and these suck shrewdly.

RICARDO [whistles]
Sir, I must fetch you off. [Aside.

UBALDO
I could tell you wonders
Of the cures he has done, but a business of import
Calls me away; but, that dispatch'd, I will
Be with you presently.

[Walks aside.

SOPHIA
There is something more,
In this, than bare suspicion.

RICARDO [comes forward]
Save you, lady;
Now you look like yourself! I have not look'd on
A lady more complete, yet have seen a madam

Wear a garment of this fashion, of the same stuff too,
One just of your dimensions: Sat the wind there, boy!

SOPHIA
What lady, sir?

RICARDO
Nay, nothing; and methinks
I should know this ruby: very good! 'tis the same.
This chain of orient pearl, and this diamond too,
Have been worn before; but much good may they do you!
Strengtn to the gentleman's back! he toil'd hard for them,
Before he got them.

SOPHIA
Why, how were they gotten?

RICARDO
Not in the field with his sword, upon my life;
He may thank his close stiletto.

[**UBALDO** hems.

Plague upon it!
Run the minutes so fast? [Aside]
Pray you, excuse my manners;
I left a letter in my chamber window,
Which I would not have seen on any terms; fie on it,
Forgetful as I am! but I'll straight attend you.

[Walks aside.

SOPHIA
This is strange. His letters said these jewels were
Presented him by the queen, as a reward
For his good service, and the trunks of clothes,
That followed them this last night, with haste made up
By his direction.

UBALDO [comes forward]
I was telling you
Of wonders, madam.

SOPHIA
If you are so skilful,
Without premeditation answer me;
Know you this gown, and these rich jewels?

UBALDO

Heaven,
How things will come out! But that I should offend you,
And wrong my more than noble friend, your husband,

(For we are sworn brothers,) in the discovery
Of his nearest secrets, I could

SOPHIA

By the hope of favour
That you have from me, out with it.

UBALDO

'Tis a potent spell
I cannot resist: Why, I will tell you, madam,
And to how many several women you are
Beholding for your bravery. This was
The wedding gown of Paulina, a rich strumpet,
Worn but a day, when she married old Gonzaga,
And left off trading.

SOPHIA

O my heart!

UBALDO

This chain
Of pearl, was a great widow's, that invited
Your lord to a masque, and the weather proving foul,
He lodged in her house all night, and merry they were;
But how he came by it, I know not.

SOPHIA

Perjured man!

UBALDO

This ring was Julietta's, a fine piece,
But very good at the sport: this diamond
Was madam Acanthe's, given him for a song
Prick'd in a private arbour, as she said,
When the queen ask'd for't; and she heard him sing too,
And danced to his hornpipe, or there are liars abroad.
There are other toys about you, the same way purchased;
But, pa'rallel'd with these, not worth the relation.
You are happy in a husband, never man
Made better use of his strength: would you have him waste
His body away for nothing? if he holds out,
There's not an embroider 'd petticoat in the court,
But shall be at your service.

SOPHIA
I commend him,
It is a thriving trade; but pray you leave me
A little to myself.

UBALDO
You may command
Your servant, madam.

[Walks aside.

She's stung unto the quick, lad.

RICARDO
I did my part: if this potion work not, hang me!
Let her sleep as well as she can to-night, tomorrow
We'll mount new batteries.

UBALDO
And till then leave her.

[Exeunt **UBALDO** and **RICARDO**.

SOPHIA
You Powers, that take into your care the guard
Of innocence, aid me! for I am a creature
So forfeited to despair, hope cannot fancy
A ransom to redeem me. I begin
To waver in my faith, and make it doubtful,
Whether the saints, that were canonized for
Their holiness of life, sinn'd not in secret;
Since my Mathias is fallen from his virtue,
In such an open fashion. Could it be, else,
That such a husband, so devoted to me,
So vow'd to temperance, for lascivious hire
Should prostitute himself to common harlots!
Old and deform'd too! Was't for this he left me,
And on a feign'd pretence, for want of means
To give me ornament? or to bring home
Diseases to me? Suppose these are false,
And lustful goats; if he were true and right,
Why stays he so long from me, being made rich,
And that the only reason why he left me?
No, he is lost; and shall I wear the spoils
And salaries of lust! they cleave unto me,
Like Nessus' poison'd shi'rt: no, in my rage,
I'll tear them off, and from my body wash

The venom with my tears. Have I no spleen,
Nor anger of a woman? shall he build
Upon my ruins, and I, unrevenged,
Deplore his falsehood? no; with the same trash
For which he had dishonour'd me, I'll purchase
A just revenge: I am not yet so much
In debt to years, nor so mis-shaped, that all
Should fly from my embraces: Chastity,
Thou only art a name, and I renounce thee t
I am now a servant to voluptuousness.
Wantons of all degrees and fashions, welcome!
You shall be entertain'd; and, if I stray,
Let him condemn himself, that led the 'way.

[Exit.

ACT IV

SCENE I. Alba Regalis. A Room in the Palace

Enter **MATHIAS** and **BAPTISTA**.

BAPTISTA
We are in a desperate strait; there's no evasion,
Nor hope left to come off, but by your yielding
To the necessity; you must feign a grant
To her violent passion, or

MATHIAS
What, my Baptista?

BAPTISTA
We are but dead else.

MATHIAS
Were the sword now heaved up,
And my neck upon the block, I would not buy
An hour's reprieve with the loss of faith and virtue,
To be made immortal here. Art thou a scholar,
Nay, almost without parallel, and yet fear
To die, which is inevitable! You may urge
The many years that, by the course of nature,
We may travel in this tedious pilgrimage,
And hold it as a blessing; as it is,
When innocence is our guide: yet know,
Baptista,

Our virtues are preferr'd before our years,
By the great Judge: to die untainted in
Our fame and reputation is the greatest;
And to lose that, can we desire to live?
Or shall I, for a momentary pleasure,
Which soon comes to a period, to all times
Have breach of faith and perjury remember 'd
In a still-living epitaph? no, Baptista,
Since my Sophia will go to her grave
Unspotted in her faith, I'll follow her
With equal loyalty:

[Takes out the picture.

But look on this,
Your own great work, your masterpiece, and then,
She being still the same, teach me to alter!
Ha! sure I do not sleep! or, if I dream,
This is a terrible vision! I will clear
My eyesight; perhaps melancholy makes me
See that which is not.

BAPTISTA
It is too apparent.
I grieve to look upon't: besides the yellow,
That does assure she's tempted, there are lines
Of a dark colour, that disperse themselves
O'er every miniature of her face, and those
Confirm

MATHIAS
She is turn'd whore!

BAPTISTA
I must not say so.
Yet, as a friend to truth, if you will have me
Interpret it, in her consent and wishes
She's false, but not in fact yet.

MATHIAS
Fact, Baptista!
Make not yourself a pander to her looseness,
In labouring to palliate what a visor
Of impudence cannot cover. Did e'er woman,
In her will, decline from chastity, but found means,
To give her hot lust fuel? It is more
Impossible in nature for gross bodies,
Descending of themselves, to hang in the air;

Or with my single arm to underprop
A falling tower; nay, in its violent course
To stop the lightning, than to stay a woman
Hurried by two furies, lust and falsehood,
In her full career to wickedness!

BAPTISTA
Pray you, temper
The violence of your passion.

MATHIAS
In extremes
Of this condition, can it be in man
To use a moderation? I am thrown,
From a steep rock, headlong into a gulph
Of misery, and find myself past hope,
In the same moment that I apprehend
That I am falling: and this, the figure of
My idol, few hours since, while she continued
In her perfection, that was late a mirror,
In which I saw miraculous shapes of duty,
Staid manners, with all excellency a husband
Could wish in a chaste wife, is on the sudden
Turn'd to a magicall glass, and does present
Nothing but horns and horror.

BAPTISTA
You may yet,
And 'tis the best foundation, build up comfort
On your own goodness.

MATHIAS
No, that hath undone me;
For now I hold my temperance a sin
Worse than excess, and what was vice, a virtue.
Have I refused a queen, and such a queen,
Whose ravishing beauties at the first sight had tempted
A hermit from his beads, and changed his prayers
To amorous sonnets, to preserve my faith
Inviolate to thee, with the hazard of
My death with torture, since she could inflict
No less for my contempt; and have I met
Such a return from thee! I will not curse thee,
Nor, for thy falsehood, rail against the sex;
'Tis poor, and common: I'll only with wise men,
Whisper unto myself, howe'er they seem,
Nor present, nor past times, nor the age to come,
Hath heretofore, can now, or ever shall,

Produce one constant woman.

BAPTISTA
This is more
Than the satirists wrote against them.

MATHIAS
There's no language
That can express the poison of these aspics,
These weeping crocodiles, and all too little
That hath been said against them. But I'll mould
My thoughts into another form; and, if
She can outlive the report of what I have done,
This hand, when next she comes within my reach,
Shall be her executioner.

[Enter **HONORIA** and **ACANTHE**.

BAPTISTA
The queen, sir.

HONORIA
Wait our command at distance:

[Exit **ACANTHE**.

Sir, you too have
Free'liberty to depart.

BAPTISTA
I know my manners,
And thank you for the favour.

[Exit.

HONORIA
Have you taken
Good rest in your new lodgings? I expect now
Your resolute answer: but advise maturely
Before I hear it.

MATHIAS
Let my actions, madam,
For no words can dilate my joy, in all
You can command, with cheerfulness to serve you,
Assure your highness; and, in sign of my
Submission, and contrition for my error,
My lips, that but the last night shunn'd the touch

Of yours as poison, taught humility now,
Thus on your foot, and that too great an honour
For such an undeserver, seal my duty.
A cloudy mist of ignorance, equal to
Cimmerian darkness, would not let me see, then,
What now, with adoration and wonder,
With reverence I look up to: but those fogs
Dispersed and scatter'd by the powerful beams
With which yourself, the sun of all perfection,
Vouchsafe to cure my blindness; like a suppliant,
As low as I can kneel, I humbly beg
What you once pleased to tender.

HONORIA
This is more
Than I could hope!
[Aside]
What find you so attractive
Upon my face, in so short time to make
This sudden metamorphosis? pray you, rise;
I, for your late neglect, thus sign your pardon.

[Kisses him,

Ay, now you kiss like a lover, and not as brothers
Coldly salute their sisters.

MATHIAS
I am turn'd
All spirit and fire.

HONORIA
Yet, to give some allay
To this hot fervour, 'twere good to remember
The king, whose eyes and ears are everywhere;
With the danger too that follows, this discover'd.

MATHIAS
Danger! a bugbear, madam; let me ride once
Like Phaeton in the chariot of your favour,
And I contemn Jove's thunder; though the king,
In our embraces stood a looker on,
His hangman, and with studied cruelty, ready
To drag me from your arms, it should not fright me
From the enjoying that a single life is
Too poor a price for. O, that now all vigour
Of my youth were re-collected for an hour,
That my desire might meet with yours, and draw

The envy of all men, in the encounter,
Upon my head! I should but we lose time
Be gracious, mighty queen.

HONORIA
Pause yet a little:
The bounties of the king, and, what weighs more,
Your boasted constancy to your matchless wife,
Should not so soon be shaken.

MATHIAS
The whole fabric,
When I but look on you, is in a moment
O'erturn'd and ruin'd; and, as rivers lose
Their names when they are swallow 'd by the ocean,
In you alone all faculties of my soul
Are wholly taken up; my wife and king,
At the best, as things forgotten.

HONORIA
Can this be?
I have gain'd my end now. [Aside.

MATHIAS
Wherefore stay you, madam?

HONORIA
In my consideration what a nothing
Man's constancy is.

MATHIAS
Your beauties make it so
In me, sweet lady.

HONORIA
And it is my glory:
I could be coy now, as you were, but I
Am of a gentler temper; howsoever,
And in a just return of what I have suffer 'd
In your disdain, with the same measure grant me
Equal deliberation: I ere long
Will visit you again; and when I next
Appear, as conquer 'd by it, slave-like wait
On my triumphant beauty.

[Exit.

MATHIAS

What a change
Is here beyond my fear! but by thy falsehood,
Sophia, not her beauty, is't denied me
To sin but in my wishes? what a frown,
In scorn, at her departure, she threw on me!
I am both ways lost; storms of contempt and scorn
Are ready to break on me, and all hope
Of shelter doubtful: I can neither be
Disloyal, nor yet honest; I stand guilty
On either part; at the worst, Death will end all;
And he must be my judge to right my wrong,
Since I have loved too much, and lived too long.

[Exit.

SCENE II. Bohemia. A Room in Mathias' House

Enter **SOPHIA**, with a book and a paper.

SOPHIA
Nor custom, nor example, nor vast numbers
Of such as do offend, make less the sin.
For each particular crime a strict account
Will be exacted; and that comfort which
The damn'd pretend, fellows in misery,
Takes nothing from their torments: every one,
Must suffer, in himself, the measure of
His wickedness. If so, as I must grant,
It being unrefutable in reason,
Howe'er my lord offend, it is no warrant
For me to walk in his forbidden paths:
What penance then can expiate my guilt,
For my consent (transported then with passion)
To wantonness? the wounds I give my fame,
Cannot recover his; and, though I have fed
These courtiers with promises and hopes,
I am yet in fact untainted; and I trust,
My sorrow for it, with my purity,
And love to goodness for itself, made powerful,
Though all they have alleged prove true or false,
Will be such exorcisms as shall Command
This Fury, jealousy, from me? What I have
Determined touching them, I am resolved
To put in execution. Within, there!

[Enter **HILARIO, CORISCA**, with other **SERVANTS**.

Where are my noble guests?

HILARIO
The elder, madam,
Is drinking by himself to your ladyship's health,
In muskadine and eggs; and, for a rasher
To draw his liquor down, he hath got a pie
Of marrowbones, potatoes, and eringos,
With many such ingredients; and, 'tis said,
He hath sent his man in post to the next town,
For a pound of ambergris, and half a peck
Of fishes call'd cantharides.

CORISCA
The younger
Prunes up himself, as if this night he were
To act a bridegroom's part; but to what purpose,
I am ignorance itself.

SOPHIA
Continue so.

[Gives the **SERVANTS** the paper.

Let those lodgings be prepared as this directs you:
And fail not in a circumstance, as you
Respect my favour.

1ST SERVANT
We have our instructions.

2ND SERVANT
And punctually will follow them.

[Exeunt **SERVANTS**.

[Enter **UBALDO**.

HILARIO
Here comes, madam,
The lord Ubaldo.

UBALDO
Pretty one, there's gold
To buy thee a new gown; [To **CORISCA**] and there's for thee;
Grow fat, and fit for service. [To **HILARIO**] I am now,
As I should be, at the height, and able to-

Beget a giant. O my better angel!
In this you shew your wisdom, when you pay
The letcher in his own coin; shall you sit puling,
Like a Patient Grizzle, and be laughed at? no:
This is a fair revenge. Shall we to't?

SOPHIA
To what, sir?

UBALDO
The sport you promised.

SOPHIA
Could it be done with safety.

UBALDO
I warrant you; I am sound as a bell, a tough
Old blade, and steel to the back, as you shall find me
In the trial on your anvil.

SOPHIA
So; but how, sir,
Shall I satisfy your friend, to whom, by promise,
I am equally engaged?

UBALDO
I must confess,
The more the merrier; but, of all men living,
Take heed of him: you may safer run upon
The mouth of a cannon when it is unlading,
And come off colder.

SOPHIA
How! is he not wholesome?

UBALDO
Wholesome! I'll tell you, for your good: he is
A spittle of diseases, and, indeed,
More loathsome and infectious; the tub is
His weekly bath: he hath not drank this seven years,
Before he came to your house, but compositions
Of sassafras and guaicum; and dry mutton
His daily portion: name what scratch soever
Can be got by women, and the surgeons will resolve you,
At this time, or at that, Ricardo had it.

SOPHIA
Bless me from him!

UBALDO
'Tis a good prayer, lady.
It being a degree unto the pox,
Only to mention him: if my tongue burn not, hang me,
When I but name Ricardo.

SOPHIA
Sir, this caution
Must be rewarded.

UBALDO
I hope I have marr'd his market,
[Aside.
But when?

SOPHIA
Why, presently; follow my woman,
She knows where to conduct you, and will serve
To-night for a page. Let the waistcoat I appointed,
With the cambric shirt perfumed, and the rich cap,
Be brought into his chamber.

UBALDO
Excellent lady!
And a caudle too in the morning.

CORISCA
I will fit you.

[Exeunt **UBALDO** and **CORISCA**.

[Enter **RICARDO**.

SOPHIA
So hot on the scent! Here comes the other beagle.

RICARDO [To **HILARIO**]
Take purse and all.

HILARIO
If this company would come often,
I should make a pretty term on't.

SOPHIA
For your sake
I have put him off; he only begg'd a kiss,
I gave it, and so parted.

RICARDO

I hope better:
He did not touch your lips?

SOPHIA

Yes, I assure you.
There was no danger in it?

RICARDO

No! eat presently
These lozenges of forty crowns an ounce,
Or you are undone.

SOPHIA

What is the virtue of them?

RICARDO

They are preservatives against stinking breath,
Rising from rotten lungs.

SOPHIA

If so, your carriage
Of such dear antidotes, in my opinion,
May render yours suspected.

RICARDO

Fie! no; I use them
When I talk with him, I should be poison'd else,
But I'll be free with you: he was once a creature,
It may be, of God's making, but long since
He is turn'd to a druggist's shop; the spring and fall
Hold all the year with him: that he lives, he owes
To art, not nature; she has given him o'er.
He moves, like the fairy king, on screws and wheels,
Made by his doctor's recipes, and yet still
They are out of joint, and every day repairing.
He has a regiment of whores he keeps,
At his own charge, in a lazar-house; but the best is,
There's not a nose among them. He's acquainted
With the green water, and the spitting pill's
Familiar to him: in a frosty morning,
You may thrust him in a pottle-pot; his bones
Rattle in his skin, like beans tossed in a bladder.
If he but hear a coach, the fomentation,
The friction with fumigation, cannot save him
From the chine-evil. In a word, he is
Not one disease, but all; yet, being my friend,

I will forbear his character, for I would not.
Wrong him in your opinion.

SOPHIA
The best is,
The virtues you bestow on him, to me
Are mysteries I know not; but, however,
I am at your service. Sirrah, let it be your care
To unclothe the gentleman, and with speed; delay
Takes from delight.

RICARDO
Good! there's my hat, sword, cloak:
A vengeance on these buttons! off with my doublet,
I dare shew my skin; in the touch you will like it better.
Prithee cut my codpiece-points, and, for this service,
When I leave them off, they are thine.

HILARIO
I'll take your word, sir.

RICARDO
Dear lady, stay not long.

SOPHIA
I may come too soon, sir.

RICARDO
No, no; I am ready now.

HILARIO
This is the way, sir.

[Exeunt **HILARIO** and **RICARDO**.

SOPHIA
I was much to blame to credit their reports
Touching my lord, that so traduce each other,
And with such virulent malice; though I presume
They are bad enough; but I have studied for them
A way for their recovery.

[A noise of clapping a door; **UBALDO** appears above in his shirt.

UBALDO
What dost thou mean, wench?
Why dost thou shut the door upon me? Ha!
My clothes are ta'en away too! shall I starve here?

Is this my lodging? I am sure the lady talk'd of
A rich cap, a perfum'd shirt, and a waistcoat;
But here is nothing but a little fresh straw,
A petticoat fora coverlet, and that torn too,
And an old woman's biggin, for a night-cap.

[Re-enter **CORISCA** below.

'Slight, 'tis a prison, or a pigsty. Ha!
The windows grated with iron! I cannot force them,
And if I leap down here, I break my neck;
I aip betray'd. Rogues! Villains! let me out;
I am a lord, and that's no common title,
And shall I be used thus?

SOPHIA
Let him rave, he's fast;
I'll parley with him at leisure.

[**RICARDO** entering with a great noise above, as fallen.

RICARDO
Zounds! have you trapdoors?

SOPHIA
The other bird's i'the cage too, let him flutter.

RICARDO
Whither aru I fallen? into hell!

UBALDO
Who makes that noise, there?
Help me, if thou art a friend.

RICARDO
A friend! I am where
I cannot help myself; let me see thy face.

UBALDO
How, Ricardo! Prithee, throw me
Thy cloak, if thou canst, to cover me; I am almost
Frozen to death.

RICARDO
My cloak! I have no breeches;
I am in my shirt, as thou art; and here's nothing
For myself but a clown's cast suit.

UBALDO

We are both undone.
Prithee, roar a little Madam!

[Re-enter **HILARIO** below, in Ricardo's clothes.

RICARDO

Lady of the house!

UBALDO

Grooms of the chamber!

RICARDO

Gentlewomen! Milkmaids!

UBALDO

Shall we be murder'd?

SOPHIA

No, but soundly punish'd,
To your deserts.

RICARDO

You are not in earnest, madam?

SOPHIA

Judge as you find, and feel it; and now hear
What I irrevocably purpose to you.
Being received as guests into my house,
And with all it afforded entertain 'd,
You have forgot all hospitable duties;
And, with the defamation of my lord,
Wrought on my woman weakness, in revenge
Of his injuries, as you fashion'd them to me,
To yield my honour to your lawless lust.

HILARIO

Mark that, poor fellows!

SOPHIA

And so far you have
Transgress 'd against the dignity of men,
Who should, bound to it by virtue, still defend
Chaste ladies' honours, that it was your trade
To make them infamous: but you are caught
In your own toils, like lustful beasts, and therefore

Hope not to find the usage of men from me:

Such mercy you have forfeited, and shall suffer
Like the most slavish women.

UBALDO
How will you use us?

SOPHIA
Ease, and excess in feeding, made you wanton.
A plurisy of ill blood you must let out,
By labour, and spare diet that way got too,
Or perish for hunger. Reach him up that distaff
With the flax upon it; though no Omphale,
Nor you a second Hercules, as I take it,
As you spin well at my command, and please me,
Your wages, in the coarsest bread and water,
Shall be proportionable.

UBALDO
I will starve first.

SOPHIA
That's as you please.

RICARDO
What will become of me now?

SOPHIA
You shall have gentler work; I have oft observed
You were proud to shew the fineness of your hands,
And softness of your fingers; you should reel well
What he spins, if you give your mind to it, as
I'll force you.
Deliver him his materials. Now you know
Your penance, fall to work; hunger will teach you:

And so, as slaves to your lust, not me, I leave you.

[Exeunt **SOPHIA** and **COSISCA**.

UBALDO
I shall spin a fine thread out now!

RICARDO
I cannot look
On these devices, but they put me in mind
Of rope-makers.

HILARIO

Fellow, think of thy task.
Forget such vanities; my livery there,
Will serve thee to work in.

RICARDO
Let me have my clothes yet;
I was bountiful to thee.

HILARIO
They are past your wearing,
And mine by promise, as all these can witness.
You have no holidays coming, nor will I work
While these, and this lasts; and so, when you please,
You may shut up your shop windows.

[Exit.

UBALDO
I am faint,
And must lie down.

RICARDO
I am hungry too, and cold, cursed women!

UBALDO
This comes of our whoring.
But let us rest as well as we can to-night,
But not o'ersleep ourselves, lest we fast tomorrow.

[They withdraw.

SCENE III. Alba Rcgalis. A Room in the Palace

Enter **LADISLAUS, HONORIA, EUBULUS, FERDINAND, ACANTHE** and **ATTENDANTS**.

HONORIA
Now you know all, sir, with the motives why
I forced him to my lodging.

LADISLAUS
I desire
No more such trials, lady.

HONORIA
I presume, sir,
You do not doubt my chastity.

LADISLAUS

I would not;
But these are strange inducements.

EUBULUS

By no means, sir.
Why, though he were with violence seized upon,
And still detain'd, the man, sir, being no soldier,
Nor used to charge his pike when the breach is open,
There was no danger in't! You must conceive, sir,
Being religious, she chose him for a chaplain,
To read old homilies to her in the dark;
She's bound to it by her canons.

LADISLAUS

Still tormented
With thy impertinence!

HONORIA

By yourself, dear sir,
I was ambitious only to o'erthrow
His boasted constancy in his consent;
But for fact, I contemn him: I was never
Unchaste in thought; I laboured to give proof
What power dwells in this beauty you admire so;
And when you see how soon it has transform'd him,
And with what superstition he adores it,
Determine as you please.

LADISLAUS

I will look on
This pageant; but

HONORIA

When you have seen and heard, sir,
The passages which I myself discover'd,
And could have kept conceal' d, had I meant basely,
Judge as you please.

LADISLAUS

Well, I'll observe the issue.

EUBULUS

How had you ta'en this, general, in your wife?

FERDINAND

As a strange curiosity; but queens

Are privileged above subjects, and 'tis fit, sir.

[Exeunt.

SCENE IV. Another Room in the Same

Enter **MATHIAS** and **BAPTISTA**.

BAPTISTA
You are much alter'd, sir, since the last night,
When the queen left you, and look cheerfully,
Your dulness quite blown over.

MATHIAS
I have seen a vision
This morning, makes it good; and never was
In such security as at this instant,
Fall what can fall: and when the queen appears,
Whose shortest absence now is tedious to me,
Observe the encounter.

[Enter **HONORIA. LADISLAUS, EUBULUS, FERDINAND**, and **ACANTHE**, with **OTHERS**, appear above.

BAPTISTA
She already is
Enter'd the lists.

MATHIAS
And I prepared to meet her.
Bapt, I know my duty.

[Going.

HONORIA
Not so, you may stay now,
As a witness of our contract.

BAPTISTA
I obey
In all things, madam.

HONORIA
Where's that reverence,
Or rather superstitious adoration,
Which, captive-like, to my triumphant beauty
You paid last night? No humble knee, nor sign

Of vassal duty! sure this is the foot,
To whose proud cover, and then happy in it,
Your lips were glued; and that the neck then offer'd,
To witness your subjection, to be trod on;
Your certain loss of life in the king's anger
Was then too mean a price to buy my favour;
And that false glow-worm fire of constancy
To your wife, extinguish 'd by a greater light
Shot from our eyes; and that, it may be, (being
Too glorious to be look'd on,) hath deprived you
Of speech and motion: but I will take off
A little from the splendour, and descend
From my own height, and in your lowness hear you
Plead as a suppliant.

MATHIAS
I do remember
I once saw such a woman.

HONORIA
How!

MATHIAS
And then
She did appear a most magnificent queen,
And, what's more, virtuous, though somewhat darken 'd
With pride, and self-opinion.

EUBULUS
Call you this courtship?

MATHIAS
And she was happy in a royal husband,
Whom envy could not tax, unless it were
For his too much indulgence to her humours.

EUBULUS
Pray you, sir, observe that touch, 'tis to the purpose;
I like the play the better for't.

MATHIAS
And she lived
Worthy her birth and fortune; you retain yet
Some part of her angelical form; but when
Envy to the beauty of another woman,
Inferior to hers, one that she never
Had seen, but in her picture, had dispersed
Infection through her veins, and loyalty,

Which a great queen, as she was, should have nourish 'd,
Grew odious to her

HONORIA
I am thunderstruck.

MATHIAS
And lust, in all the bravery it could borrow
From majesty, howe'er disguised, had ta'eu
Sure footing in the kingdom of her heart,
The throne of chastity once, how, in a moment,
All that was gracious, great, and glorious in her,
And won upon all hearts, like seeming shadows
Wanting true substance, vanish'd!

HONORIA
How his reasons
Work on my soul!

MATHIAS
Retire into yourself;
Your own strengths, madam, strongly mann'd with virtue,
And be but as you were, and there's no office
So base, beneath the slavery that men
Impose on beasts, but I will gladly bow to.
But as you play and juggle with a stranger,
Varying your shapes like Thetis, though the beauties
Of all that are by poets' raptures sainted
Were now in you united, you should pass
Pitied by me, perhaps, but not regarded.

EUBULUS
If this take not, I am cheated.

MATHIAS
To slip once,
Is incident, and excused by human frailty;
But to fall ever, damnable. We were both
Guilty, I grant, in tendering our affection;
But, as I hope you will do, I repented.
When we are grown up to ripeness, our life is
Like to this magick picture. While we run
A constant race in goodness, it retains
The just proportion; but the journey being
Tedious, and sweet temptation in the way,
That may in some degree divert us from
The road that we put forth in, ere we end
Our pilgrimage, it may, like this, turn yellow,

Or be with blackness clouded: but when we
Find we have gone astray, and labour to
Return unto our never-failing guide,
Virtue, contrition, with unfeigned tears,
The spots of vice wash'd off, will soon restore it
To the first pureness.

HONORIA
I am disenchanted:
Mercy, O mercy, heavens!

[Kneels.

LADISLAUS
I am ravish'd
With what I have seen and heard.

FERDINAND
Let us descend,
And hear the rest below.

EUBULUS
This hath fallen out
Beyond my expectation.

[They retire.

HONORIA
How have I wander'd
Out of the track of piety! and misled
By overweening pride, and flattery
Of fawning sycophants, (the bane of greatness,)
Could never meet till now a passenger,
That in his charity would set me right,
Or stay me in my precipice to ruin.
How ill have I retura'd your goodness tome!
The horror, in my thought oft, turns me marble:
But if it may be yet prevented

[Re-enter **LADISLAUS**, **EUBULUS**, **FERDINAND**, **ACANTHE**, and **OTHERS**, below.

O sir,
What can I do to shew my sorrow, or
With what brow ask your pardon?

LADISLAUS
Pray you, rise.

HONORIA
Never, till you forgive me, and receive
Unto your love and favour a changed woman:
My state and pride turn'd to humility, henceforth
Shall wait on your commands, and my obedience
Steer'd only by your will.

LADISLAUS
And that will prove
A second and a better marriage to me.
All is forgotten.

HONORIA
Sir, I must not rise yet,
Till, with a free confession of a crime
Unknown to you yet, and a following suit,
Which thus I beg, be granted.

LADISLAUS
I melt with you:
'Tis pardon'd, and confirm'd thus.

[Raises her.

HONORIA
Know then, sir,
In malice to this good knight's wife, I practised
Ubaldo and Ricardo to corrupt her.

BAPTISTA [Aside]
Thence grew the change of the picture.

HONORIA
And how far
They have prevail'd, I am ignorant: now, if you, sir,
For the honour of this good man, may be entreated
To travel thither, it being but a day's journey,
To fetch them off

LADISLAUS
We will put on to-night.

BAPTISTA
I, if you please, your harbinger.

LADISLAUS
I thank you.
Let me embrace you in my arms; your service

Done on the Turk, compared with this, weighs nothing.

MATHIAS
I am still your humble creature.

LADISLAUS
My true friend.

FERDINAND
And so you are bound to hold him.

EUBULUS
Such a plant
Imported to your kingdom, and here grafted,
Would yield more fruit than all the idle weeds
That suck up your rain of favour.

LADISLAUS
In my will
I'll not be wanting. Prepare for our journey.

[Exeunt.

ACT V

SCENE I. Bohemia. A Hall in Mathias House

Enter **SOPHIA**, **CORISCA**, and **HILARIO**.

SOPHIA
Are they then so humble?

HILARIO
Hunger and hard labour
Have tamed them, madam; at the first they bellow'd
Like stags ta'en in a toil, and would not work
For sullenness; but when they found, without it,
There was no eating, and that, to starve to death,
Was much against their stomach; by degrees,
Against their wills, they fell to it.

CORISCA
And now feed on
The little pittance you allow, with gladness.

HILARIO

I do remember that they stopp'd their noses
At the sight of beef and mutton, as coarse feeding
For their fine palates; but now, their work being ended,
They leap at a barley crust, and hold cheese-parings,
With a spoonful of pall'd wine pour'd in their water,
For festival-exceedings.

CORISCA
When I examine
My spinster's work, he trembles like a prentice,
And takes a box on the ear, when I spy faults
And botches in his labour, as a favour
From a curst-mistress.

HILARIO
The other, too, reels well
For his time; and if your ladyship would please
To see them for your sport, since they want airing,
It would do well, in my judgment; you shall hear
Such a hungry dialogue from them!

SOPHIA
But suppose,
When they are out of prison, they should grow
Rebellious?

HILARIO
Never fear't; I'll undertake
To lead them out by the nose with a coarse thread
Of the one's spinning, and make the other reel after,
And without grumbling; and when you are weary of
Their company, as easily return them.

CORISCA
Dear madam, it will help to drive away
Your melancholy.

SOPHIA
Well, on this assurance,
I am content; bring them hither.

HILARIO
I will do it
In stately equipage.

[Exit.

SOPHIA

They have confess'd, then,
They were set on by the queen, to taint me in
My loyalty to my lord?

CORISCA
'Twas the main cause,
That brought them hither.

SOPHIA
I am glad I know it;
And as I have begun, before I end
I'll at the height revenge it; let us step aside,
They come: the object's so ridiculous,
In spite of my sad thoughts, I cannot but lend
A forced smile to grace it.

[Re-enter **HILARIO**, with **UBALDO** spinning, and **RICARDO** reeling.

HILARIO
Come away:
Work as you go, and lose no time, 'tis precious;
You'll find it in your commons.

RICARDO
Commons, call you it!
The word is proper; I have grazed so long
Upon your commons, I am almost starv'd here.

HILARIO
Work harder, and they shall be better'd.

UBALDO
Better'd!
Worser they cannot be: would I might lie
Like a dog' under her table, and serve for a footstool,
So I might have my belly full of that
Her Iceland cur refuses!

HILARIO
How do you like
Your airing? is it not a favour?

RICARDO
Yes;
Just such a one as you use to a brace of greyhounds,
When they are led out of their kennels to scumber;
But our case is ten times harder, we have nothing
In our bellies to be vented: if you will be

An honest yeoman-fewterer, feed us first,
And walk us after.

HILARIO
Yeoman-fewterer!
Such another word to your governor, and you go upperless to bed for't.

UBALDO
Nay, even as you please;
The comfortable names of breakfasts, dinners,
Collations, supper, beverage, are words
Worn out of our remembrance.

RICARDO
O for the steam
Of meat in a cook's shop!

UBALDO
I am so dry
I have not spittle enough to wet my fingers
When I draw my flax from my distaff.

RICARDO
Nor I strength
To raise my hand to the top of my reeler. Oh!
I have the cramp all over me.

HILARIO
What do you think
Were best to apply to it? A cramp-stone, as I take it,
Were very useful.

RICARDO
Oh! no more of stones,
We have been used too long like hawks already.

UBALDO
We are not so high in our flesh now to need casting,
We will come to an empty fist.

HILARIO
Nay, that you shall not.
So ho, birds!

[Holds -up a piece of bread?

How the eyasses scratch and scramble!
Take heed of a surfeit, do not cast your gorges;

This is more than I have commission for; be thankful.

SOPHIA
Were all that study the abuse of women,
Used thus, the city would not swarm with cuckolds,
Nor so many tradesmen break.

CORISCA
Pray you, appear now,
And mark the alteration.

[**SOPHIA** comes forward.

HILARIO
To your work,
My lady is in presence; shew your duties:
Exceeding well.

SOPHIA
How do your scholars profit?

HILARIO
Hold up your heads demurely.
Prettily,
For young beginners.

CORISCA
And will do well in time,
If they be kept in awe.

RICARDO
In awe! I am sure
I quake like an aspen leaf.

UBALDO
No mercy, lady?

RICARDO
Nor intermission?

SOPHIA
Let me see your work:
Fie upon't, what a thread's here! a poor cobbler's wife
Would make a finer to sew a clown's rent startup;
And here you reel as you were drunk.

RICARDO
I am sure

It is not with wine.

SOPHIA
O take, heed of wine;
Cold water is far better for your healths,
Of which I am very tender: you had foul bodies,
And must continue in this physical diet,
Till the cause of your disease be ta'en away,
For fear of a relapse; and that is dangerous:
Yet I hope already that you are in some
Degree recover'd, and that way to resolve me,
Answer me truly; nay, what I propound
Concerns both; nearer: what would you now give,
If your means were in your hands, to lie all night
With a fresh and handsome lady?

UBALDO
How! a lady?
O, I am past it; hunger with her razor
Hath made me an eunuch.

RICARDO
For a mess of porridge,
Well sopp'd with a bunch of radish and a carrot,
I would sell my barony; but for women, oh!
No more of women; not a doit for a doxy,
After this hungry voyage.

SOPHIA
These are truly odd symptoms; let them not venture too much in the air,
Till they are weaker.

RICARDO
This is tyranny.

UBALDO
Scorn upon scorn.

SOPHIA
You were so
In your malicious intents to me,

[Enter a **SERVANT**.

And therefore 'tis but justice
What's the business?

SERVANT

My lord's great friend, signior
Baptista, madam,
Is newly lighted from his horse, with certain
Assurance of my lord's arrival.

SOPHIA
How?
And stand I trifling here? Hence with the mongrels
To their several kennels; there let them howl in private;
I'll be no further troubled.

[Exeunt **SOPHIA** and **SERVANT**.

UBALDO
O that ever
I saw this fury!

RICARDO
Or look'd on a woman
But as a prodigy in nature!

HILARIO
Silence;
No more of this.

CORISCA
Methinks you have no cause
To repent your being here.

HILARIO
Have you not learnt,
When your states are spent, your several trades to live by,
And never charge the hospital?

CORISCA
Work but tightly,
And we will not use a dish-clout in the house,
But of your spinning.

UBALDO
O, I would this hemp
Were turn'd to a halter!

HILARIO
Will you march?

RICARDO
A soft one,

Good general, I beseech you.

UBALDO
I can hardly
Draw my legs after me.

HILARIO
For a crutch, you may use
Your distaff; a good wit makes use of all things.

[Exeunt.

SCENE II. A Room in the Same

Enter **SOPHIA** and **BAPTISTA**.

SOPHIA
Was he jealous of me?

BAPTISTA
There's no perfect love
Without some touch oft, madam.

SOPHIA
And my picture,
Made by your devilish art, a spy upon
My actions! I ne'er sat to be drawn,
Nor had you, sir, commission for't.

BAPTISTA
Excuse me;
At his earnest suit I did it.

SOPHIA
Very good:
Was I grown so cheap in his opinion of me?

BAPTISTA
The prosperous events that crown his fortunes,
May qualify the offence.

SOPHIA
Good, the events!
The sanctuary fools and madmen fly to,
When their rash and desperate undertakings thrive well:
But good and wise men are directed by

Grave counsels, and with such deliberation
Proceed in their affairs, that chance has nothing
To do with them: howsoe'er, take the pains, sir,
To meet the honour (in the king and queen's
Approaches to my house) that breaks upon me;
I will expect them with my best of care.

BAPTISTA
To entertain such royal guests

SOPHIA
I know it;
Leave that to me, sir.

[Exit **BAPTISTA**.

What should move the queen,
So given to ease and pleasure, as fame speaks her,
To such a journey! or work on my lord,
To doubt my loyalty, nay, more, to take,
For the resolution of his fears, a course
That is by holy writ denied a Christian?
'Twas impious' in him, and perhaps the welcome
He hopes in my embraces, may deceive

[Trumpets sounded.

His expectation. The trumpets speak
The king's arrival: help, a woman's wit now,
To make him know his fault, and my just anger!

[Exit.

SCENE III. A Hall in the Same

A Flourish.

[Enter **LADISLAUS, FERDINAND, EUBULUS, MATHIAS, BAPTISTA, HONORIA**, and **ACANTHE**, with
ATTENDANTS.

EUBULUS
Your majesty must be weary.

HONORIA
No, my lord,
A willing mind makes a hard journey easy.

MATHIAS
Not Jove, attended on by Hermes, was
More welcome to the cottage of Philemon,
And his poor Baucis, than your gracious self,
Your matchless queen, and all your royal train,
Are to your servant and his wife.

LADISLAUS
Where is she?

HONORIA
I long to see her as my now-loved rival.

EUBULUS
And I to have a smack at her; 'tis a cordial
To an old man, better than sack and a toast
Before he goes to supper.

MATHIAS
Ha! is my house turn'd
To a wilderness? Nor wife nor servants ready,
With all rites due to majesty, to receive
Such unexpected blessings! You assured me
Of better preparation; hath not
The excess of joy transported her beyond
Her understanding?

BAPTISTA
I now parted from her,
And gave her your directions.

MATHIAS
How shall I beg
Your majesties' patience! sure my family's drunk,
Or by some witch, in envy of my glory,
A dead sleep thrown upon them.

[Enter **HILARIO** and **SERVANTS**.

SERVANT
Sir.

MATHIAS
But that
The sacred presence of the king forbids it,
My sword should make a massacre among you.
Where is your mistress?

HILARIO
First, you are welcome home, sir:
Then know, she says she's sick, sir. There's no notice
Taken of my bravery! [Aside.

MATHIAS
Sick at such a time!
It cannot be: though she were on her deathbed,
And her spirit e'en now departed, here stand they
Could call it back again, and in this honour,
Give her a second being. Bring me to her;
I know not what to urge, or how to redeem
This mortgage of her manners.

[Exeunt **MATHIAS**, **HILARIO**, and **SERVANTS**.

EUBULUS
There's no climate
On the world, I think, where one jade's trick or other
Reigns not in women.

FERDINAND
You were ever bitter
Against the sex.

LADISLAUS
This is very strange.

HONORIA
Mean women
Have their faults, as well as queens.

LADISLAUS
O, she appears now.

[Re-enter **MATHIAS** with **SOPHIA**; **HILARIO** following.

MATHIAS
The injury that you conceive I have done you
Dispute hereafter, and in your perverseness
Wrong not yourself and me.

SOPHIA
I am past my childhood,
And need no tutor.

MATHIAS

This is the great king,
To whom I am engaged till death for all
I stand possess'd of.

SOPHIA
My humble roof is proud, sir,
To be the canopy of so much greatness
Set off with goodness.

LADISLAUS
My own praises flying
In such pure air as your sweet breath, fair lady,
Cannot but please me.

MATHIAS
This is the queen of queens,
In her magnificence to me.

SOPHIA
In my duty
I kiss her highness' robe.

HONORIA
You stoop too low
To her whose lips would meet with yours.

[Kisses her.

SOPHIA
Howe'er
It may appear preposterous in women,
So to encounter, 'tis your pleasure, madam,
And not my proud ambition. Do you hear, sir?
Without a magical picture, in the touch
I find your print of close and wanton kisses
On the queen's lips. [Aside to **MATHIAS**.

MATHIAS
Upon your life be silent:
And now salute these lords.

SOPHIA
Since you will have me,
You shall see I am experienced at the game,
And can play it tightly. You are a brave man, sir, [To **FERDINAND**]
And do deserve a free and hearty welcome:
Be this the prologue to it.

[Kisses him.

EUBULUS
An old man's turn
Is ever last in kissing. I have lips too,
However cold ones, madam.

SOPHIA
I will warm them
With the fire of mine.

[Kisses him.

EUBULUS
And so she has! I thank you,
I shall sleep the better all night for't.

MATHIAS
You express
The boldness of a wanton courtezan,
And not a matron's modesty; take up,
Or you are disgraced for ever.

[Aside to **SOPHIA**

SOPHIA
How? with kissing
Feelingly, as you taught me? would you have me
Turn my cheek to them, as proud ladies use
To their inferiors, as if they intended
Some business should be whisper'd in their ear,
And not a salutation? what I do,
I will do freely; now I am in the humour,
I'll fly at all: are there any more?

MATHIAS
Forbear,
Or you will raise my anger to a height
That will descend in fury.

SOPHIA
Why? you know
How to resolve yourself what my intents are,
By the help of Mephostophilus, and your picture:
Pray you, look upon't again. I humbly thank
The queen's great care of me while you were absent.
She knew how tedious 'twas for a young wife,
And being for that time a kind of widow,

To pass away her melancholy hours
Without good company, and in charity, therefore,
Provided for me: out of her own store,
She cull'd-the lords Ubaldo and Ricardo,
Two principal courtiers for ladies' service,
To do me all good offices; and as such
Employ'd by her, I hope I have received
And entertain'd them; nor shall they depart,
Without the effect arising from the cause
That brought them hither.

MATHIAS
Thou dost belie thyself:
I know that in my absence thou wert honest,
However now turn'd monster.

SOPHIA
The truth is,
We did not deal, like you, in speculations
On cheating pictures; we knew shadows were
No substances, and actual performance
The best assurance. I will bring them hither,
To make good in this presence so much for me.
Some minutes space I beg your majesties' pardon.
You are moved now: champ upon this bit a little,
Anon you shall have another. Wait me,
Hilario.

[Exeunt **SOPHIA** and **HILARIO**.

LADISLAUS
How now? turn'd statue, sir!

MATHIAS
Fly, and fly quickly,
From this cursed habitation, or this Gorgon
Will make you all as I am. In her tongue
Millions of adders hiss, and every hair
Upon her wicked head a snake more dreadful,
Than that Tisiphone threw on Athamas,
Which in his madness forced him to dismember
His proper issue. O that ever I
Reposed my trust in magick, or believed
Impossibilities! or that charms had power
To sink and search into the bottomless hell
Of a false woman's heart!

EUBULUS

These are the fruits
Of marriage! an old bachelor as I am,
And, what's more, will continue so, is not troubled
With these fine vagaries.

FERDINAND
Till you are resolv'd, sir,
Forsake not hope.

BAPTISTA
Upon my life, this is
Dissimulation.

LADISLAUS
And it suits not with
Your fortitude and wisdom, to be thus
Transported with your passion.

HONORIA
You were once
Deceived in me, sir, as I was in you;
Yet the deceit pleased both.

MATHIAS
She hath confess'd all;
What further proof should I ask?

HONORIA
Yet remember
The distance that is interposed between
A woman's tongue and her heart; and you must grant,
You build upon no certainties.

[Re-enter **SOPHIA**, **CORISCA**, and **HILARIO**, with **UBALDO** and **RICARDO** in rags, and spinning and reeling, as before.

EUBULUS
What have we here?

SOPHIA
You must come on, and shew yourselves.

UBALDO
The king!

RICARDO
And queen too! would I were as far under the earth
As I am above it!

UBALDO
Some poet will,
From this relation, or in verse or prose,
Or both together blended, render us
Ridiculous to all ages.

LADISLAUS
I remember
This face, when it was in a better plight:
Are not you Ricardo?

HONORIA
And this thing, I take it,
Was once Ubaldo.

UBALDO
I am now I know not what.

RICARDO
We thank your majesty for employing us
To this subtle Circe.

EUBULUS
How, my lord! turn'd spinster!
Do you work by the day, or the great?

FERDINAND
Is your theorbo
Turn'd to a distaff, signior? and your voice,
With which you chanted, Room for a lusty gallant!
Tuned to the note of Lachrynuz?

EUBULUS
Prithee tell me,
For I know thou'rt free, how oft, and to the purpose,
You've been merry with this lady.

RICARDO
Never, never.

LADISLAUS
Howsoever, you should say so for your credit,
Being the only court-bull.

UBALDO
O, that ever
I saw this kicking heifer!

SOPHIA

You see, madam,
How I have cured your servants, and what favours,
They, with their rampant valour, have won from me.
You may, as they are physic'd, I presume,
Trust a fair virgin with them; they have learn'd
Their several trades to live by, and paid nothing
But cold and hunger for them; and may now-
Set up for themselves, for here I give them over.
And now to you, sir; why do you not again.
Peruse your picture, and take the advice
Of your learned consort? these are the men, or none,
That make you, as the Italian says, a becco.

MATHIAS

I know not which way to entreat your pardon,
Nor am I worthy of it. My Sophia,
My best Sophia, here before the king,
The queen, these lords, and all the lookers on;
I do renounce my error, and embrace you,
As the great example to all aftertimes,
For such as would die chaste and noble wives,
With reverence to imitate.

SOPHIA

Not so, sir;
I yet hold off. However I have purged
My doubted innocence, the foul aspersions,
In your unmanly doubts, cast on my honour,.
Cannot so soon be wash'd oft".

EUBULUS

Shall we have
More jiggobobs yet!

SOPHIA

When you went to the wars,
I set no spy upon you, to observe
Which way you wander'd, though our sex by nature
Is subject to suspicions and fears;
My confidence in your loyalty freed me from them.
But, to deal, as you did, against your religion,
With this enchanter, to survey my actions,
Was more than woman's weakness; therefore know,
And 'tis my boon unto the king, I do
Desire a separation from your bed;
For I will spend the remnant of my life

In prayer and meditation.

MATHIAS
O take pity
Upon my weak condition, or I am
More wretched in your innocence, than if
I had found you guilty. Have you shewn a jewel
Out of the cabinet of your rich mind,
To lock it up again? She turns away.
Will none speak for me? shame and sin have robb'd me
Of the use of my tongue.

LADISLAUS
Since you have conquer'd, madam,
You wrong the glory of your victory,
If you use it not with mercy.

FERDINAND
Any penance
You please to impose upon him, I dare warrant
He will gladly suffer.

EUBULUS
Have I lived to see
But one good woman, and shall we for a trifle,
Have her turn nun? I will first pull down the cloister.
To the old sport again, with a good luck to you!
Tis not alone enough that you are good,
We must have some of the breed of you: will you destroy
The kind and race of goodness? I am converted,
And ask your pardon, madam, for my ill opinion
Against the sex; and shew me but two such more,
I'll marry yet, and love them.

HONORIA
She that yet
Ne'er knew what 'twas to bend but to the king,
Thus begs remission for him.

SOPHIA
O, dear madam,
Wrong not your greatness so.

OMNES
We are all suitors.

UBALDO
I do deserve to be heard among the rest.

RICARDO
And we have suffer'd for it.

SOPHIA
I perceive
There's no resistance: but, suppose I pardon
What's past, who can secure me he'll be free
From jealousy hereafter?

MATHIAS
I will be
My own security; go, ride, where you please;
Feast, revel, banquet, and make choice with whom,
I'll set no watch upon you; and, for proof of it,
This cursed picture I surrender up
To a consuming fire.

BAPTISTA
As I abjure
The practice of my art.

SOPHIA
Upon these terms
I am reconciled; and, for these that have paid
The price of their folly, I desire your mercy.

LADISLAUS
At your request they have it.

UBALDO
Hang all trades now!

RICARDO
I will find a new one, and that is, to live honest.

HILARIO
These are my fees.

UBALDO
Pray you, take them, with a mischief!

LADISLAUS
So, all ends in peace now.
And, to all married men, be this a caution,
Which they should duly tender as their life,
Neither to dote too much, nor doubt a wife.

[Exeunt.

PHILIP MASSINGER — A SHORT BIOGRAPHY

This biography was initially written in 1830

Very few materials exist for a life of Massinger beyond the entries of the Parish Register or the College Books, and a few slender intimations scattered here and there in the dedications to his plays. From these scanty sources the following brief memoir is derived.

Our author was born at Salisbury in the year 1584: he was the son of Arthur Massinger, a gentleman in the service of Henry, the second Earl of Pembroke. We must not suppose, from his being thus attached to the family of a nobleman, that the father of our poet was a person of inferior birth and station. In those days the word servant carried with it no sense of degradation. The great lords and officers of the court numbered inferior nobles among their followers. We read, in Cavendish's Life of Wolsey, that "my Lord Percy, the son and heir of the Earl of Northumberland, attended upon and was servitor to the lord-cardinal:" and from the situation which Arthur Massinger held in the household of so high and influential a person as the Earl of Pembroke, we might be justly led to argue rather favourably than unfavourably of his family and his connexions. "There were," says Mr. Gifford, "many considerations which united to render this state of dependance respectable and even honourable. The secretaries, clerks, and assistants, of various departments, were not then, as now, nominated by the government, but left to the choice of the person who held the employment; and as no particular dwelling was officially set apart for their residence, they were entertained in the house of their principal. That communication, too, between noblemen of power and trust, both of a public and private nature, which is now committed to the post, was in those days managed by confidential servants, who were despatched from one to the other, and even to the sovereign;" and, indeed, the father of our poet himself was, we know, in one instance thus employed as the bearer of communications from his patron to Elizabeth. We read in The Sidney Letters, "Mr. Massinger is newly come up from the Earl of Pembroke with letters to the queen for his lordship's leave to be away this St. George's Day." This was an errand which would not have been intrusted to the execution of any inconsiderable person: unimportant as the occasion may appear to us, it would not have been regarded in that light by Elizabeth; for no monarch ever exacted from the nobility, and particularly from her officers of state, a more rigid and scrupulous compliance with stated order than this princess.

With regard to the early youth of Massinger, we possess no information whatever. Mr. Gifford supposes that it might have been passed at Wilton, a seat belonging to the Earl of Pembroke, in the neighbourhood of Salisbury; but this mode of disposing of his early years rests on a very improbable conjecture. It may occasionally have happened that the child of a favourite dependant was admitted as the companion of the younger branches of the patron's family, and allowed to receive his education among them; but this was certainly not an ordinary case; and, like Cavendish, a large majority of the great man's servants and dependants "left wife and children, home and family, rest and quietness, only to serve him."—Massinger was most likely educated at the grammar-school of Salisbury, where many distinguished characters have received the rudiments of their education, among whom the elegant and accomplished Addison is to be numbered. But wherever the first years of our poet's life may have been spent, and whatever may have been the nature of his education, we know that at the age of eighteen (May 14, 1602) he was entered at the university of Oxford, and became a commoner of St. Alban's Hall.

Massinger resided at Oxford about four years, and then abruptly left it, without taking any degree. The cause of this sudden departure is ascribed by Mr. Gifford to the death of his father, from whom his supplies were derived: but Davies relates a very different story, and asserts that the Earl of Pembroke, who had sent him to the university and maintained him there, withdrew the necessary allowance in consequence of his having misapplied the time demanded for severer studies, in the pursuit of a more attractive but less profitable description of literature. Each opinion is equally ungrounded on the basis of any substantial evidence, and rests almost entirely on the imagination of the biographer: what slight authority there is favours the latter supposition, which, perhaps, on the whole, is most consistent with the known circumstances of the case. Anthony Wood, who was born, lived, and died at Oxford; who spent his time in collecting and recording the gossip which circulated in the university respecting the characters and conduct of its more distinguished sons; and whose evidence, however indifferent it may be, is the best that can be obtained upon the subject, confirms the representation of Davies:— "Massinger," says Wood, "gave his mind more to poetry and romance, for about four years or more, than to logic and philosophy, which he ought to have done, as he was patronised to that end." This passage corroborates the account of Davies so far as to intimate that patronage was afforded to our author, and that cause of dissatisfaction was given to the patron; but it goes no farther: it does not even state to whom the poet was indebted for assistance, nor that the misapplication of his academic hours was at all resented by the friend from whom the assistance was received: but still Wood is very probably correct in his information that other than his paternal funds were depended upon for maintaining Massinger at the university; and if such was the case, there can be no question from whose hands they must have proceeded; while the simple fact of his having been totally neglected, from the time of his father's death, by the whole of the Pembroke family, till after the demise of the earl, carries with it a strong suspicion that some offence was committed on the side of the poet, and tenaciously remembered on the side of the peer. Henry, the second Earl of Pembroke, died (1601) the year before Massinger was admitted at Oxford; and William, the third earl, to whom the father of Massinger continued attached during life, is universally and justly considered one of the brightest ornaments of the courts of Elizabeth and James. He was a man of generous and liberal disposition; the distinguished patron of arts and learning; and a lover of poetry, which he himself cultivated with some degree of success. It is not probable—it is impossible—that such a man should have allowed the highly talented son of an old and faithful servant of his family to be checked in his course of study, and abandoned to maintain, through the early years of life, a single-handed contest with adversity, for the want of that pecuniary aid which he could have yielded and never missed, unless some strong and decided cause of displeasure had existed. Had Massinger been merely forced to leave the university, as Mr. Gifford supposes, because the funds necessary to maintain him there had failed with the life of his father, we impute an act of illiberality to the Earl of Pembroke which is inconsistent with the whole tenor of his life and character. From whatever source the expenses of our author's education were originally defrayed, their suddenly ceasing argues in favour of the account intimated by Wood and detailed by Davies. If his father had, during his life, supported him at the university, there must have been some reason for the earl's not continuing that support when the father of Massinger was no more; and perhaps the most honourable supposition for both parties is that which represents the earl as offended by the bent of our author's studies and pursuits. By adopting this view of the case we are saved from the painful necessity of either assuming, on the one hand, that a nobleman distinguished among the most amiable characters of his age allowed a highly gifted and meritorious young man, a natural dependant of his house, to languish in the want of that countenance and protection on which he had an hereditary claim; or, on the other hand, that Massinger had incurred the displeasure of his natural and hereditary patron by the commission of some more crying offence.

Every, even the slightest, surmise of Mr. Gifford is deserving attention and respect; but I cannot admit the supposition by which he would account for the alienation that subsisted between the Earl of Pembroke and our author. That distinguished critic has inferred, from the religious sentiments contained in The Virgin Martyr, that Massinger was a Roman catholic, and for that cause neglected by the protector of his father. But if the intimations scattered through this play and others should be received as sufficient evidence of the faith of Massinger, we must, on similar evidence—the intimations contained in Measure for Measure, for instance—conclude that the religion of Shakspeare was the same; and then we are cast back upon our old difficulty, and have to explain why William Earl of Pembroke, a celebrated patron of literary men, and of dramatists in particular, scorned to yield his notice to the catholic Massinger, while (to use the expression of Heminge and Condell) he "prosequuted" the catholic Shakspeare and "his works with so much favour?" There are many reasons for believing Shakspeare to have been a member of the church of Rome; and the patronage afforded him by the Earl of Pembroke proves, that that nobleman extended his liberality to men of genius without any regard to distinctions of faith; but, on the other hand, we have no just grounds for assuming that Massinger really did hold the same opinions. The only evidence we have upon this point, that afforded by the general tone of his writings, is of a most vague and superficial description. What, in fact, can be inferred from it? We may from such a source derive very satisfactory information respecting the sentiments which would be favourably received by the audience, but very little respecting those of the author. The truth is, that though the national religion was reformed in its liturgy and articles, the feelings, prejudices, and superstitions of the people were still almost entirely catholic; and Massinger, like any other dramatic author, writing for the amusement of the people, necessarily addressed them in a language they would understand, and with sentiments that accorded with their own. Besides, as a poet, he would never carry his theological distinctions to his literary labours: Voltaire himself is catholic in his tragedies; and Massinger naturally adopted the creed which was most suitable to the purposes of poetry, and afforded the most picturesque ceremonies and romantic situations. I feel inclined, therefore, to dismiss entirely the theory suggested by Mr. Gifford, for these two reasons; first, supposing our author to have been a catholic, we have no reason for condemning the Earl of Pembroke as a bigot and a persecutor, who would close his eyes to the merits of so great an author, because his faith did not tally with his own; and, secondly, we have no sufficient grounds for supposing him to have been a catholic at all. But with regard to all such visionary conjectures, thinking is literally a waste of thought.

Whatever may have been the nature of Massinger's studies at Oxford, it is quite certain, from the general character of his works, that his time could not have been wasted there; and his literary acquirements, at the period of his leaving the university, appear to have been multifarious and extensive. He was about two-and-twenty (1606) when he arrived in London, where, as he more than once observes, he was driven by his necessities, and somewhat inclined, perhaps, by the peculiar bent of his talents, to dedicate himself to the service of the stage.

The theatre, when Massinger first took up his abode in the metropolis, must have presented attractions of all others the most calculated to excite the interest, and inspire the imagination, of a young man of sensibility, taste, and education like our poet. No art ever attained a more rapid maturity than the dramatic art in England. The people had, indeed, been long accustomed to a species of exhibition, called MIRACLES or MYSTERIES, founded on sacred subjects, and performed by the ministers of religion themselves, on the holy festivals, in or near the churches, and designed to instruct the ignorant in the leading facts of sacred history. From the occasional introduction of allegorical characters, such as Faith, Death, Hope, or Sin, into these religious dramas, representations of another kind, called MORALITIES, had by degrees arisen, of which the plots were more artificial, regular, and connected, and which were entirely formed of such personifications: but the first rough draught of a regular tragedy and comedy—Lord Sackville's Gorboduc, and Still's Gammer Gurton's Needle—were not produced till within the latter half of the sixteenth century, and little more than twenty years before the stage acquired its highest splendour in the productions of Shakspeare.

About the end of the sixteenth century, the attention of the public began to be more generally directed to the drama; and it throve most admirably beneath the cheering beams of popular favour. The theatrical performances which in the early part of Elizabeth's reign had been exhibited on temporary stages, erected in such halls or apartments as the actors could procure, or, more generally, in the yards of the larger inns, while the spectators surveyed them from the surrounding windows and galleries, began to find more convenient and permanent habitations. About the year 1569, a regular playhouse, under the appropriate name of The Theatre, was erected. It is supposed to have stood somewhere in Blackfriars; and, three years after the commencement of this establishment, the queen, yielding to her own inclination for such amusements, and disregarding the remonstrances of the Puritans, granted licence and authority to the servants of the Earl of Leicester ("for the recreation of her loving subjects, as for her own solace and pleasure when she should think good to see them") to exercise their occupation throughout the whole realm of England. From this time the number of theatres increased with the increasing demands of the people. Various noblemen had their respective companies of performers, who were associated as their servants, and acted under their protection; and when Massinger left Oxford, and commenced dramatic author, there were no less than seven principal theatres open in the metropolis.

With respect to the interior arrangements, there were very few points of difference between our modern theatres and those of the days of Massinger. The prices of admission, indeed, were considerably cheaper: to the boxes the entrance was a shilling; to the pit and galleries only sixpence. Sixpence also was the price paid for stools upon the stage; and these seats, as we learn from Decker's Gull's Hornbook, were particularly affected by the wits and critics of the time. The conduct of the audience was less restrained by the sense of public decorum, and smoking tobacco, playing at cards, eating and drinking, were generally prevalent among them. The hours of performance were also earlier: the play commencing at one o'clock. During the representation a flag was unfurled at the top of the theatre; and the stage, according to the universal practice of the age, was strewn with rushes; but, in all other respects, the theatres of Elizabeth and James's days seem to have borne a perfect resemblance to our own. They had their pit, where the inferior class of spectators, the groundlings, vented their clamorous censure or approbation; they had their boxes—rooms as they were called—to which the right of exclusive admission was engaged by the night, for the more affluent portion of the audience; and there were again the galleries, or scaffoldings above the boxes, for those who were content to purchase less commodious situations at a cheaper rate. On the stage, in the same manner, the appointments appear to have been nearly of the same description as at present. The curtain divided the audience from the actors, which, at the third sounding, not indeed of the bell, but of the trumpet, was drawn for the commencement of the performance. Malone, in his account of the ancient theatre, supposes that there were no moveable scenes; that a permanent elevation of about nine feet was raised at the back of the stage, from which, in many of the old plays, part of the dialogue was spoken; and that there was a private box on each side this platform. Such an arrangement would have destroyed all theatrical illusion; and it seems extraordinary that any spectators should desire to fix themselves in a station where they could have seen nothing but the backs and trains of the performers; but, as Malone himself acknowledges the spot to have been inconvenient, and that "it is not very easy to ascertain the precise situation where these boxes really were", it may very reasonably be presumed, that they were not placed in the position that the historian of the English stage has supposed. As to the permanent floor, or upper stage, of which he speaks, he may or may not be correct in his statement. All that his quotations upon the subject really establish is, that in the old, as in the modern theatre, when the actor was to speak from a window, or balcony, or the walls of a fortress, the requisite ingenuity was not wanting to contrive a representation of the place. But with regard to the use of painted moveable scenery, it is not possible, from the very circumstances of the case, to believe him correct in his theory. Such a contrivance could not have escaped our ancestors. All the materials were ready to their hands. They had not to invent for themselves, but merely to adapt an old invention to that peculiar purpose; and at a time when every better-furnished apartment was adorned with tapestry; when even the rooms of the commonest taverns were hung with painted cloths; while all the materials were constantly before their eyes, we can hardly believe our forefathers to have been so deficient in ingenuity, as to have missed the simple contrivance of converting the common ornaments of their walls into the decorations of their theatres. But, in fact, the use of scenery was almost co-existent with the introduction of dramatic representations in this country. In the Chester Mysteries (1268), the most ancient and complete collection of the kind which we possess, is found the following stage direction: "Then Noe shall go into the arke with all his familye, his wife excepte. The arke must be boarded round about; and upon the boardes all the beastes and fowles, hereafter rehearsed, must be painted, that their wordes may agree with their pictures." In this passage we have a clear reference to a painted scene. It is not likely that, in the lapse of three centuries, while all other arts were in a state of rapid improvement, and the art of dramatic writing, perhaps, more rapidly and successfully improved than any other, the art of theatrical decoration should have alone stood still. It is not improbable that their scenes were few; and that they were varied, as occasion might require, by the introduction of different pieces of stage furniture. Mr. Gifford, who adheres to the opinions of Malone, says, "A table with a pen and ink thrust in, signified that the stage was a counting-house; if these were withdrawn and two stools put in their place, it was then a tavern." And this might be perfectly satisfactory as long as the business of the play was supposed to be passing within doors; but when it was removed to the open air, such meagre devices would no longer be sufficient to guide the imagination of the audience, and some new method must have been adopted to indicate the place of action. After giving the subject very considerable attention, I cannot help thinking that Steevens was right in rejecting Malone's theory, and concluding that the spectators were, as at the present day, assisted in following the progress of the story by means of painted moveable scenery. This opinion is confirmed by the ancient stage directions. In the folio Shakspeare, 1623, we read "Enter Brutus in his orchard; Enter Timon in the woods; Enter Timon from the cave." In Coriolanus, "Marcius follows them to the gates and is shut in." Innumerable instances of the same kind might be cited to prove that the ancient stage was not so defective in the necessary decorations as some antiquaries of great authority would represent. "It may be added," says Steevens, "that the dialogue of our old dramatists has such perpetual reference to objects supposed visible to the audience, that the want of scenery could not have failed to render many of the descriptions absurd. Banquo examines the outside of Inverness castle with such minuteness, that he distinguishes even the nests which the martens had built under the projecting part of its roof. Romeo, standing in a garden, points to the tops of fruit-trees gilded by the moon. The prologue speaker to the second part of Henry the Fourth expressly shows the spectators 'This worm-eaten hold of ragged stone,' in which Northumberland was lodged. Iachimo takes the most exact inventory of every article in Imogen's bed-chamber, from the silk and silver of which her tapestry was wrought, down to the Cupids that support her andirons. Had not the inside of the apartment, with its proper furniture, been represented, how ridiculous must the action of Iachimo have appeared! He must have stood looking out of the room for the particulars supposed to be visible within it." The works of Massinger would afford innumerable instances of a similar kind to vindicate the opinion which Steevens has asserted on the testimony of Shakspeare alone. But on this subject there is one passage which appears to me quite conclusive. Must not all the humour of the mock play in The Midsummer Night's Dream have been entirely lost, unless the audience before whom it was performed were accustomed to all the embellishments requisite to give effect to a dramatic representation, and could consequently estimate the absurdity of those shallow contrivances and mean substitutes for scenery devised by the ignorance of the clowns?

In only one respect do I perceive any material difference between the mode of representation at the time of Massinger and at present: in his day, the female parts were performed by boys. This custom, which must in many cases have materially injured the illusion of the scene, was in others of considerable advantage: it furnished the stage with a succession of youths, regularly educated for the art, to fill, in every department of the drama, the characters suited to their age. When the lad had become too tall for Juliet, he had acquired the skill, and was most admirably fitted, both in age and appearance, for performing the part which Garrick considered the most difficult on the stage, because it needed "an old head upon young shoulders," the ardent and arduous character of Romeo. When the voice had "the mannish crack," that rendered the youth unfit to appear as the representative of the gentle Imogen, the stage possessed in him the very person that was wanting to do justice to the princely sentiments of Arviragus or Guiderius.

Such was the state of the stage when Massinger arrived in the metropolis, and dedicated his talents to its service. He joined a splendid fraternity, for Shakspeare, Jonson, Beaumont, Fletcher, Shirley, were then flourishing at the height of their reputation, and the full vigour of their genius. Massinger came among them no unworthy competitor for such honours and emoluments as the theatre could afford. Of the honours, indeed, he seems to have reaped a very fair and equitable portion; of the emoluments, the harvest was less abundant. In those days, very little pecuniary reward was to be gained by the dramatic poet, unless, as indeed was most frequently the case, he added the profession of the actor to that of the author, and recited the verses which he wrote. The distinguished performers of that time, Alleyn, Burbage, Heminge, Condell, Shakspeare, all appear to have died in independent, if not affluent, circumstances; but the remuneration obtained by the poet was most miserably curtailed. The price given at the theatre for a new play fluctuated between ten and twenty pounds; the copyright, if the piece was printed, might produce from six to ten pounds more; in addition to these sums, the dedication-fee may be reckoned, the usual amount of which was forty shillings. Our author appears to have produced about two or three plays every year. Most of them were successful; but, even with this industry and good fortune, his annual income would rarely have exceeded fifty pounds: and we cannot, therefore, feel surprised at finding him continually speaking of his necessities; or that the only existing document connected with his life should be one that represents him in a state of pecuniary embarrassment.

Among the papers of Dulwich College, the indefatigable Mr. Malone discovered the following letter tripartite, which, coming from persons of such deserved celebrity, cannot fail of interesting the reader.

"To our most loving friend, Mr. Phillip Hinchlow, esquire, these.

"Mr. Hinchlow,

"You understand our unfortunate extremitie, and I doe not thincke you so void of Christianitie but that you would throw so much money into the Thames as wee request now of you, rather than endanger so many innocent lives. You know there is xl. more, at least, to be receaved of you for the play. We desire you to lend us vl. of that, which shall be allowed to you; without which, we cannot be bayled, nor I play any more till this be dispatch'd. It will lose you xxl. ere the end of the next weeke, besides the hindrance of the next new play. Pray, sir, consider our cases with humanity, and now give us cause to acknowledge you our true freind in time of neede. Wee have entreated Mr. Davison to deliver this note, as well to witness your love as our promises, and alwayes acknowledgement to be ever

"Your most thankfull and loving friends,
"NAT. FIELD."

"The money shall be abated out of the money remayns for the play of Mr. Fletcher and ours.
"ROB. DABORNE."

"I have ever found you a true loving friend to mee, and in soe small a suite, it beinge honest, I hope you will not fail us.
"PHILIP MASSINGER."

Indorsed.
"Received by mee, Robert Davison, of Mr. Hinchlow, for the use of Mr. Daboerne, Mr. Feeld, Mr. Messenger, the sum of vl.
"ROB. DAVISON."

The occasion of the distress in which these three distinguished persons were involved it is not possible to fathom. We may imagine a thousand emergencies, either creditable or discreditable to the fame of the writers, with which the letter would perfectly tally; but, on such slight and vague intimations, no ingenuity could determine which was most likely to be correct. But from the document a circumstance is ascertained, which, before its discovery, had been called in question. Sir Aston Cockayne, a friend of Massinger, had asserted in a volume of poems, published in 1658, that our author had written in conjunction with Fletcher; Davies doubted this report, but the above letter establishes the fact beyond the possibility of dispute.

Massinger is known to have produced thirty-seven plays for the stage, a list of which is given at the conclusion of this memoir. Sixteen entire plays and the fragment of another, The Parliament of Love, alone are extant. No less than eleven of his productions, in manuscript, were in possession of Mr. Warburton (Somerset Herald), and destroyed with the rest of that gentleman's invaluable collection by his cook, who, ignorant of their worth, used them as waste paper for the purposes of the kitchen.

The great and various merits of the works of Massinger will be better seen in the following volumes than in any elaborate, critical dissertation. If our author be compared with the other dramatic writers of his age, we cannot long hesitate where to place him. More natural in his characters and more poetical in his diction than Jonson or Cartwright, more elevated and nervous than Fletcher, the only writers who can be supposed to contest his pre-eminence, Massinger ranks immediately under Shakspeare himself. Our poet excels, perhaps, more in the description than in the expression of passion; this may in some measure be ascribed to his attention to the fable: while his scenes are managed with consummate skill, the lighter shades of character and sentiment are lost in the tendency of each part to the catastrophe. The melody, force, and variety of his versification are always remarkable. The prevailing beauties of his productions are dignity and elegance; their predominant fault is want of passion.

Massinger's last play—which is unfortunately lost—The Anchoress of Pausilippo, was acted Jan. 26, 1640, about six weeks before his death, which happened on the 17th of March, 1640. He went to bed in good health, says Langbaine, and was found dead in the morning, in his own house on the Bankside. He was buried in the churchyard of St. Saviour's, and the comedians paid the last sad duty to his name, by attending him to the grave.

It does not appear, though every stone and every fragment of a stone has been carefully examined, that any monument or inscription of any kind marked the place where his dust was deposited. "The memorial of his mortality," says Gifford, "is given with a pathetic brevity, which accords but too well with the obscure and humble passages of his life: March 20, 1639-40, buried Philip Massinger, A STRANGER."

Such is all the information that remains to us of this distinguished poet. But though we are ignorant of every circumstance respecting him but that he lived, wrote, and died, we may yet form some idea of his personal character from the recommendatory poems prefixed to his several plays, in which, as Mr. Gifford justly observes, the language of his panegyrists, though warm, expresses an attachment apparently derived not so much from his talents as his virtues: he is their beloved, much-esteemed, dear, worthy, deserving, honoured, long-known, and long-loved friend. All the writers of his life represent him as a man of singular modesty, gentleness, candour, and affability; nor does it appear that he ever made or found an enemy.

PHILIP MASSINGER – A CONCISE BIBLIOGRAPHY

As would be expected many works from this time no longer exist either in part or their entirety. Further many playwrights collaborated on plays or revised them for later performances and we have used the latest position known on each of them for the bibliography below.

Solo Plays
The Maid of Honour, tragicomedy (c. 1621; printed 1632)
The Duke of Milan, tragedy (c. 1621–3; printed 1623, 1638)
The Unnatural Combat, tragedy (c. 1621–6; printed 1639)
The Bondman, tragicomedy (licensed 3 December 1623; printed 1624)
The Renegado, tragicomedy (licensed 17 April 1624; printed 1630)
The Parliament of Love, comedy (licensed 3 November 1624; MS)
A New Way to Pay Old Debts, comedy (c. 1625; printed 1632)
The Roman Actor, tragedy (licensed 11 October 1626; printed 1629)
The Great Duke of Florence, tragicomedy (licensed 5 July 1627; printed 1636)
The Picture, tragicomedy (licensed 8 June 1629; printed 1630)
The Emperor of the East, tragicomedy (licensed 11 March 1631; printed 1632)
Believe as You List, tragedy (rejected by the censor in January, but licensed 6 May 1631; MS)
The City Madam, comedy (licensed 25 May 1632; printed 1658)
The Guardian, comedy (licensed 31 October 1633; printed 1655)
The Bashful Lover, tragicomedy (licensed 9 May 1636; printed 1655)

Collaborations with John Fletcher
Sir John van Olden Barnavelt, tragedy (August 1619; MS)
The Little French Lawyer, comedy (c. 1619–23; printed 1647)
A Very Woman, tragicomedy (c. 1619–22; licensed 6 June 1634; printed 1655)
The Custom of the Country, comedy (c. 1619–23; printed 1647)

The Double Marriage, tragedy (c. 1619–23; Printed 1647)
The False One, history (c. 1619–23; printed 1647)
The Prophetess, tragicomedy (licensed 14 May 1622; printed 1647)
The Sea Voyage, comedy (licensed 22 June 1622; printed 1647)
The Spanish Curate, comedy (licensed 24 October 1622; printed 1647)
The Lovers' Progress or The Wandering Lovers, tragicomedy (licensed Dec 1623; rev 1634; printed 1647)
The Elder Brother, comedy (c. 1625; printed 1637).

Collaborations with John Fletcher and Francis Beaumont
Thierry and Theodoret, tragedy (c. 1607; printed 1621)
The Coxcomb, comedy (1608–10; printed 1647)
Beggars' Bush, comedy (c. 1612–15; revised 1622; printed 1647)
Love's Cure, comedy (c. 1612–15; revised 1625; printed 1647).

Collaborations with John Fletcher and Nathan Field
The Honest Man's Fortune, tragicomedy (1613; printed 1647)
The Queen of Corinth, tragicomedy (c. 1616–18; printed 1647)
The Knight of Malta, tragicomedy (c. 1619; printed 1647).

Collaborations with Nathan Field
The Fatal Dowry, tragedy (c. 1619, printed 1632); adapted by Nicholas Rowe: The Fair Penitent

Collaborations with John Fletcher, John Ford, and William Rowley, or John Webster
The Fair Maid of the Inn, comedy (licensed 22 January 1626; printed 1647).

Collaborations with John Fletcher, Ben Jonson, and George Chapman
Rollo Duke of Normandy, or The Bloody Brother, tragedy (c. 1616–24; printed 1639).

Collaborations with Thomas Dekker
The Virgin Martyr, tragedy (licensed 6 October 1620; printed 1622).

Collaborations with Thomas Middleton and William Rowley
The Old Law, comedy (c. 1615–18; printed 1656).